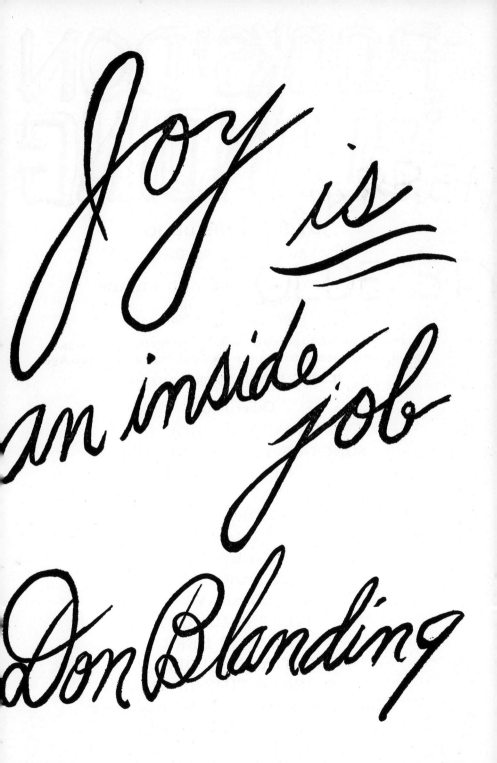

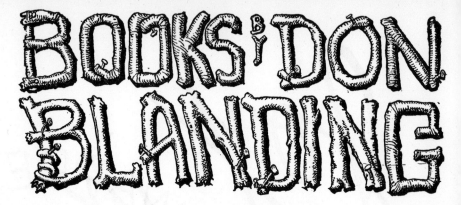

BOOKS BY DON BLANDING

JOY IS AN INSIDE JOB

An Informal Guide Book
for
THE JOYOUS JOURNEY TO JOY-AGE
Whatever your Age,
Your Joy-Age Is Now

Poems, pictures, parables, puzzles, pointers, pass-alongs,
ponder-overs and patrin in the Idiom of the Land of Joy-Age

ILLUSTRATIONS BY THE AUTHOR

Other Books

VAGABOND'S HOUSE
SONGS OF THE SEVEN SENSES
HULA MOONS
STOWAWAYS IN PARADISE
MEMORY ROOM
LET US DREAM
DRIFTER'S GOLD
THE REST OF THE ROAD
FLORIDAYS
PILOT BAILS OUT
TODAY IS HERE
MOSTLY CALIFORNIA
A GRAND TIME LIVING
BRIEF APRILS by Edythe Hope Genée
Illustrated by Don Blanding

JOY
IS AN INSIDE JOB

by Don Blanding

ILLUSTRATIONS BY THE AUTHOR

DODD, MEAD & COMPANY · NEW YORK · 1958

Frontispiece photograph by Lonnie Hull

PRINTED IN THE UNITED STATES OF AMERICA
BY THE VAIL-BALLOU PRESS, INC., BINGHAMTON, N. Y.

CONTENTS

[7]

GRATEFULNESS TO . . .

YOU. Yes, *you*. Because *you* are in this page of expression of the rich warming emotion of Gratefulness which I feel toward all who helped with this book. . . . *"What did I do?"* you ask.
Perhaps you gave friendliness . . . or understanding silence,
    perhaps expectancy . . . or patient listening,
        perhaps you were simply *there* when I needed you,
        or when I needed the thought of you
            as *you,* Companion Vagabond,
            as I think of you,
                are here now.
The shy, courteous Micronesian crew of the Motor Vessel METOM-KIN.
The generous, helpful people of Pacific Micronesian Line, Inc.
The Trust Territory folks who opened the way for my voyage to the Islands Beyond Yesterday, Micronesia.
The hospitality and comradeship of my friends of Bend, Oregon.
The loyalty and enthusiastic understanding of Revisers.
Encouragement of Companion Vagabonds of the Search for Truth in the Centers of the West . . . *I name you in my heart where there is room.*
The Staff of the *Science of Mind* Magazine. The Staff of *Let's Live.*
The folks of *Center of Light* and *Gusto.*
The patience and encouragement of friends of Dodd, Mead and Company
The Haven of Ed and Carmen Sawtelle's home during many years.
You whose names I never knew who helped pass hours on planes, buses, ships and trains with friendly exchange of talk and confidences.
As the list extends on to the never-vanishing point, I realize that
I must give All-Inclusive Thanks to Creative God for the splendid, beautiful and sometimes terrifying World We Live In, where I found
    JOY.
        MAHALO NUI OE   and   ALOHA

To TED NARRAMORE, friend, companion and guide to high adventure at intervals over twenty years, most recently as Captain of the MV METOMKIN, a freighter of the Pacific Micronesian Line, Inc., Agana Guam, M.I., in voyages among the Islands Beyond Yesterday, Micronesia, with names straight out of the Jabberwocky Dictionary: Yap, Koror, Palau, Babelthaup, Saipan, Pagan, Ulithi, Majuro, where people live in Space-Without-Time,* insulated by vast distances from Time-As-We-Know-It in our speed-driven, greed-riven, unshriven Contemporary World, and isolated by Delayed-Time from awareness of the frenzied and clamorous insistencies of gadget-ridden Babylon-Of-Today.

Mahalo nui oe,† Ted, for steering me into Three Adventures in One World or One Adventure in Three Worlds,* or maybe a combination of both.

With gratitude which might be partly expressed but never repaid, I dedicate this book to you,

Aloha,

* Key Words and Patrin used throughout the Joyous Journey to Joy-Age will be found in *Idiom of Joy-Age* through the pages.

† *Mahalo nui oe* . . . In Hawaiian, *"Thank you very much."*

WHERE IS VAGABOND'S HOUSE NOW?

Vagabond's House has been four times a House of Wood and Stone.
Between times it is a Dream House built around Memory Room.
Vagabond's House is *"whatever I am whenever I am wherever I am."*
  address, *Vagabond's House, Open Road,*
        State of Happiness, Universe, Unlimited. *N.M.A.
        *N.M.A. means *"No Mailing Address."*
During the uncomfortable period when I was not certain whether my
unease and restlessness were caused by gas or inspiration for *"JOY
IS AN INSIDE JOB,"* Vagabond's House was definitely *on the move.*
        Vagabond's House, Follywood Blvd. & Babylon Road,
        Hollywood, State of Exhilaration, California. N.M.A.
For quite a period of mingled delight and distress it was . . .
        Vagabond's House, Cypress Shadows, % Rip Tides,
        Carmel-by-the-Sea, California. N.M.A.
Then for a splendid year-and-a-half it was happily located at
        Vagabond's House, Bend of the River Deschutes,
        Oregon, on the Dawn Side of the Cascades,
        Where The Vast Horizontals of the Desert
        Meet The Inspiring Verticals of the Mountains
    With The Silver Thread of a River to Bind Them Together, N.M.A.
For two months on the freighter MV METOMKIN I visited the Islands of Micronesia, yipping on Yap, careening on Koror, simmering
on Saipan and mooning on Majuro with other Jabberwockian diversions
and fun.
        Then the address was . . .

      →

Vagabond's House, ooo Flying Fish Lane,
Islands Beyond Yesterday, Micronesia,
Pacific, Unmited, % Trade Winds, N.M.A.
Now it is a studio in a Chinese Courtyard in Hawaiian Islands . . .
Vagabond's House, Court of the Considered Lily,
Languor Lane, Honolulu, Aloha Land, Hawaiian Islands,
N.M.A.
Where next? Wouldn't want to know if I could. The Element of the
Unexpected makes Vagabond's House suitable to my raffish kind of life.
Drop in some day . . . if you can find it. . . .
Vagabond's House, West of the Sunset
and East of the Dawn . . . N.M.A.

**** **** **** ****

A CERTAIN HOUR

*Sometimes it seems that we live our entire lives to reach the climax and crisis
of "A Certain Hour." When we learn the Source of Joy we find we can pattern
the Heaven of our Skies with these Star-Moments.*

You gave a perfect hour into my hands,
    Frost-frail to shatter with a moth-wing's buffet.
I did not clutch nor cling, and so, Thank God,
    I did not muff it.

My hands are empty, yet the empty curves
    Are warmly brimmed, yes, brimmed and overflowing.
How did I know to hold with open palms
    What holding would have lost me, all unknowing?

*This reads like a love poem. In a larger significance it is one. The story of it is in
the poem, "I Died at Dawn." You'll come to it later. Don't look it up now. Please.*

ALOHA, FRIENDS

"Aloha" is both Greeting and Farewell in my long-time home, Hawaii.
I may be saying "Aloha" in both senses. That's up to you.
Some folks will say, *"Omigod, he's talking about God!"*
Some will say, *"The fellow is finding himself at last. I'm glad."*
Some will say, *"If that raffish Vagabond has found peace, healing
and a new Joy-of-Living through Cosmic or Spiritual Values . . .
maybe there's something in it for me."*

Letters carrying the last two statements started coming in fast
after *Pilot Bails Out, Today Is Here, Mostly California* and
A Grand Time Living. They're still coming in asking, *"What hap-
pened?"*
    Authors know that sometimes books take over
    and insist on being something quite different
    from the original intent. That's what happened.
SILENT PARTNER insisted that I try to answer those questions . . .
    "What did you find out?"
      "Were you really healed?"
      "Is it available to me?"
      "Give us the inside story."
This *is* the inside story . . . told in the only way that I can tell it . . .
    poems . . . pictures . . . parables . . . paradoxes . . .
    pass-alongs . . . ponder-overs . . . pointers. . . .
A Parable is like a slice of bread . . . the one who chews it and digests
it gets the sustenance. Otherwise it's just another story.
    A Puzzle is fun only if you solve it yourself.
    A Paradox lets you see the inside of the outside.
    I was sick of body . . . and I was healed.
    I was weary of mind . . . and I was refreshed.
    I was ill in spirit . . . and I was renewed.
I have been frank with you on this page. This page sets the pace.

RELUCTANT AUTHOR

I didn't have the idea of doing this book. The idea *had* me.
    The idea was like an amorous octopus.
If I got loose from seven tentacles I found that the eighth one had me by the wrist, ankle or neck. I knew how the Laocoön boys felt.
    The idea was like an unburped burp . . .
I couldn't get it out of my system, and couldn't rest until I did.
I was so tangled up, gummed up, wrapped up, fouled up and wrought up
    that I felt like a frog on fly-paper
    or a kitten in a basket of yarn
    or a man making out an income-tax return.
Finally, I had a long talk with Silent Partner. *Who is Silent Partner?*
    If you haven't found your own Silent Partner
    this explanation will sound like whimsy-whamsy;
    if you have found your own Silent Partner
    I won't need to explain. *But I will . . . later.*
That's the way with authors . . . they say that something is "beyond words"
and then go ahead and use all the words they can crowd onto a page.

HERE IS THE BULL-SESSION THAT I HAD
WITH SILENT PARTNER

D.B. *"Why* do I have to do this book which I can't do?"
S.P. "You like to pay your debts . . . with interest. You have a great debt.
    If you pay your debts to men,
    what about your debt to Creative God?"
D.B. "But who am I, of all people, to talk about God in any way?"
S.P. "Listen, Son, the Prodigal Son spoke with the authority of experience. He learned about Home by leaving it and longing for it.
    He learned about Babylon by loving it, loathing it and leaving it.
    He learned more about Home by returning to it after absence.
    The Son-Who-Stayed-Home didn't know what he had while he had it."
D.B. "Oh."
S.P. "You were a man sick and weary in heart, mind and body.
    You were healed. You felt that your previous rich varied life had been only *preparation for living.* Don't you want to pass that along to others who *might be* as *you were?"*

[15]   →

D.B. "Yes, of course, but it was an intimate inner experience. It was as tremendous and definite as lightning, and as intangible as fog. I try to explain . . . and the music goes 'round and 'round . . . and comes out *nowhere*."

S.P. "Tell what happened . . . in your own words. That which happened *to* and *within* you can happen *to* and *within* others. In your earlier books you infected people who had not been to Hawaii with the 'feeling' of Hawaii and the desire to go there. They went. They *experienced Hawaii for themselves*. Tell people how it feels to be well and joy-filled after being sick, weary and lost. Pass-along your Road-Maps to your Joyous Journey to Joy-Age."

D.B. "As simple as that?"

S.P. "As simple as that."

D.B. "I'll try . . . but I'm scared pink . . . and blue . . . and green."

S.P. "That's good. You won't say anything that you *don't* mean. You'll *mean* what you *say*. And, *somehow, you'll say what you mean*."

D.B. "But where will I begin?"

S.P. "At the beginning. *What* happened *where* and *when* and *how?*"

D.B. "Maybe I'd better begin with THE THREE ATOM BOMBS THAT FELL ON VAGABOND'S HOUSE."

S.P. "It's your book. I'll stand by. But you tell it . . . begin this way . . .

Once upon a time there was a Prodigal Son who was a vaga-bond . . .

Go on from there. . . ."

D.B. "All right. A vagabond, according to the dictionary, is a '*worthless fellow*.' He is '*one who wanders from place to place, having no fixed dwelling, or if he has one, not abiding in it.*' "

This Prodigal Son was a Vagabond and a "*worthless fellow*" because somehow he couldn't place much "*worth*" on most of the things of John Ego Adamsmith's world of tangibles. And he couldn't stay in one place because somehow he *knew* that *somewhere* there was *something bigger, finer* and *more wonderful* than *anything* he had *ever known*. . . .

THAT is the beginning of the story. . . ."

GREETINGS, COMPANION VAGABONDS

From
Vagabond's House, 000 Flying Fish Lane, Islands Beyond Yesterday, Pacific,
Unlimited, Micronesia, % Trade Winds. Note: *Since this is not an address recog-*
nized by the P.O., use for friendly thoughts only.

When Vagabond meets Vagabond
Along the Trail that leads beyond
The River's Bend behind the Hill,
They rest a while within the still
Cool shade of trees and talk a bit
In Friendliness . . . or simply sit
Until the Quiet Spell is broken
By questions-answers, gestured, spoken,
Of Roads Ahead and Short-Cut Trails
Until the golden sunlight pales.
They talk of Beauty Spots to see,
Of Detours Passed. With ribaldry
And zestful mirth they ease the ache
And callouses that Journeys make.
   When Twilight dims the Afterglow
   Of Sunset Fires, slowly they go
   Their Separate Ways . . . but not Alone . . .
   Companioned by the Friendship grown
   Through Give-and-Take of Drifters' Talk.
   Lighter the Winding Roads they walk
   Because they know that Others seek
   The Misted Goal behind the Peak.
The Peak! I've glimpsed the Goal behind it.
These Road-Maps, Friend, may help *you* find it.
I *know* it's there. It's name is Joy.
So long. Good Luck. Aloha oe.
Through Sun and Snow and Driving Rain . . . Aloha 'til we meet again.

Among "Aloha's" many meanings is "Love to you."
I say it in all sincerity, Companion Vagabond.

YOU AND I ARE BEING INTRODUCED

This Book is introducing us.

It is saying, *"Vagabond, meet a Companion-Vagabond."*

I say, *"I hope that we can be friends."*

I hope that you say, *"Why not?"*

Perhaps you say, *"Oh, I've met you before through Vagabond's House or Drifter's Gold or The Rest of the Road."*

I say, *"But that was before B.T.A.B.F.O.V.H."*

You say, *"What does that mean?"*

I say, *"Before Three Atom Bombs Fell On Vagabond's House."*

So, you and I are talking. The advantage is yours.

You can shut me up at any time by closing the book.

I can't shut ME up.   You say, *"Why not?"*

I say, *"I went through an experience which you and every other person is going to experience, one way or another, sometime in his life."*

It was terrible and splendid.

I wouldn't have missed it for anything in the world.

Perhaps my experience may help you in your crisis.

Sooner or later your Joyous Veritable Self must emerge from the envelope of the Personal Seeming-Self in which you and I spend most of our bewildered demi-frustrated lives. It is a *process* like hatching, sprouting or birthing.

Strain, anxiety, fear and tenseness retard and obstruct the birth of a child. Strain, anxiety, fear and tenseness retard and obstruct the emergence of your Joyous Veritable Self into your Joy-Age.

Take it easy. Take it naturally. It is growth.

[18]

HOW THE FIRST ATOM BOMB FELL ON
VAGABOND'S HOUSE

"Joy Is An Inside Job" was written in an attempt to keep a promise. Vagabond's House is a Dream House, yet the only house I ever owned with the power to grow again of its own Power-of-Dreams. Its timbers were badly termited in 1942 when I joined the Army as a Buck-Private. I had gone from Private to Second Lieutenant in First World War. It seemed a good progression to repeat. I wanted to know what the young-sters were thinking.

Aunt Cally used to say, "Be mighty keerful what you
prays for *because you might git it."* I got.

As Acting-Sergeant at Fort Ontario, New York, during Basic Training and as an older, gray-haired man, substantially built (a polite way of saying over-weight), I was presumed to know answers.

Maybe so, but some furtive doubts were inclined to gnaw in the
woodwork like mice in the quiet hours of the night, disturbingly.

One evening a young G.I. waylaid me in barracks to ask,

"Sarge, may I ask you a very personal question?"

He was going out to the South Pacific or Europe or maybe to Africa.

He was thinking, possibly a little frightened.

He had heard his father's generation discuss War.

He had seen News Reels. He had seen Documentary Films. *He had
thought.*

Certainly he had questions. He wanted no hooey, no evasions.

"Sarge," he said. His young voice was disciplined to a quiet level,
"What do you think of this God Business?"

That's when the First Atom Bomb Fell On Vagabond's House, shattering its flimsy structure of half-answers, rationalizations, evasions.

What *did* I think of this God Business?

It was not just *his* question.

It was *my* question.

It was my question which I had evaded so long . . . my mouse in the
timbers.

The young G.I. had potential years ahead even under the threat of War.

I had . . . *how many swift decreasing years?*

The question wouldn't shrug off.

A wave of chill shame drenched me. From my years of rich living I had taken no blue-prints, no roadmaps to offer in this Crisis.

Oh, there were the shabby cynicisms of the 20's,
the brittle philosophies of the 30's,
the confused clamors of the 40's,
the clever word-patterns, philosophies and psychological speculations.

I had chewed these paper answers. They were indigestible.

"You ask me what I think," I said. *"I haven't thought."*

A smog of disappointment clouded his clear eyes.

"Oh, I've *thought* that I thought," I said, "but that's confetti. I need the answers worse than you do. In the high crisis of War maybe you'll find answers. I'm caught in the dull routine of War-on-the-Home-Front."

The young G.I. wouldn't release me. He was Fate-in-Khaki.

My shame and inner alarm made an inarticulate crying-out in my heart.

I think that I prayed . . . but not in words.

"I promise you," I said . . . and I seemed to hear the rustle of winged witnesses, *"that I will not quit searching, asking, questioning until I have found some answers. When I find answers which seem to answer I'll put them into a book. Maybe you'll find it somewhere. Maybe the answers will serve you, too.   I promise."*

It is not an easy promise to keep.

Poets are supposed to be exhibitionists.

Perhaps I am. It's not important.

It is not easy to do an emotional, personal and spiritual strip-tease showing all of the vaccination marks and scars of living.

Yet to refrain would be impossible. A promise was given.

These answers have brought me what I have sought unknowingly . . . peace.

I call this peace "dynamic serenity" . . . deep waters flowing stilly.

There are times when the surface is ruffled.

But the deep waters flow . . . still.

HUSKS AT THE BANQUET

In a cynical moment I summed up my new enthusiasm about like this:

WHEN WE'RE YOUNG AND WIND-BLOWN
We go *out* for Romance and Adventure.
WHEN WE'RE BLOWN AND WINDY
We go *in* for Philosophy and Faith.

"You've tried everything else," I told myself, "now you're getting a thrill out of religion. You're going to tell other people NOT to do what you're tired of doing. *It won't last long."*
"Could be," myself replied. *"Could be a flash enthusiasm. We'll see."*
    I had always had the curiosity of seven alley cats,
    combined with the foolhardiness of my curiosities. My slogan . . .
"I want what I want when I want it . . . and I want it NOW."
By 1942 I had most of the things which I had been sure would give me happiness, security and a constant joy-of-living. I had more than plenty of money and enough publicity to pass for what our Contemporary Age calls "Fame." I was thing-ridden with Ming, Whing, Ding and Woolworth treasure-and-trash. I had sung the Sense Songs lustily.
    But it wasn't a mere whim that sent the Prodigal Son home.
    The taste of husks is a dark brown taste.
There is no Chlorophyl of the Senses to remove the flavor.
I found the husks at the Banquet Table in the form of satiety, boredom with too-much-of-a-muchness, the ability to *get* but no capacity to *want* the things of Babylon. I was feeding a tapeworm. My hunger increased with what I fed it. Hunger for *what?* That was my question.
    I always had Faith . . . mostly in the wrong things.
    Now I have Faith which comes from the conviction of experience.
    I had always wanted to believe in God, or A God or Something
    Real in a confusing and terrifying world where everything that
    we valued, loved or seemed to own was subject to destruction,
    theft, loss or disintegration. Now I *know* . . . which passes *Belief.*
    Life *used to seem* as tricky as a Slot Machine.
    We put nickels, dimes and dollars of our days into it
    hoping to hit the Jack-Pot. Maybe we hit the Jack-Pot.
    So what? We spent it or lost it

or hoarded it and got no use from it.
But we didn't get our time-money back.
Our prizes seemed to be Bubble-Gum . . . they *chewed out* fast.
I wanted *something lasting*. I found it . . . or it *found me*.
By the judgment of John Ego Adamsmith's world, I didn't deserve it.
I soon found that there's nothing wrong with the Real World.
But the Real World is not the one that John Ego Adamsmith sees.
There was a lot wrong with Wrong-Way Blandingan
who tried to go forward by flying backward.
It was a long job righting Wrong-Way Blandingan. It climaxed right
where it began . . . *within*. I'm a run-of-the-mill person. I doubt if
you are a Great Aching Brain, a Towering Intellect or a Sainted Soul
so . . . what worked for me (and with me) will probably work for you.
I couldn't accept the religious beliefs of my time and place
in the form that they were offered. I mistook the Teachers
for the Teachings, the Gift-Wrappings for the Gift; the capsule
concealed the vitamins.   I realize that now.
I couldn't accept the pictures of God, Spirit, Jesus, Christ, Heaven,
Soul and Spiritual Things in General . . . *as they were presented*.
        Did I say *"presented?"*
My generation knows that *"presented"* is an understatement.
We youngsters were like calves, roped, thrown and tied.
We were branded with fiery irons of fanaticism,
or worse, we were sprayed with a weak solution of sentimentality,
superstition, or blistered with hellfireandbrimstone.
We were curried with the comb of dogma, which was often cat-and-
dogma.
We were fenced in with barbed-wire moralities.
Life was a monotone of "don'ts."
I *couldn't* accept these presentations . . . *in my heart where it counts*.
I couldn't *"see"* God as an Absentee Landlord
who opened a sub-division called Earth
and leased it to bewildered Man at a terrible price
of painful birth, insecure life and certain death.

→

I couldn't *"see"* God as an Oriental Despot
tyrannical and moody, jealous and vengeful,
who had to be propitiated with horrible sacrifices
and abject grovelings and bribes and gifts.
 I couldn't *"see"* God as a Grim Truant Officer
 who spent his time peeking in keyholes
 to see what small boys were doing . . . which they usually were.
Nor could I *"see"* God as an icy Principle
impersonal and mechanical as gravity
to be *used* like electricity.
  I just plain couldn't *"see"* God,
  no matter how hard I tried . . .
  and I did try.
I tried everything to fill that uneasy emptiness of heart,
 places, people, things . . . far places and near places.
 I felt that I was giving blood-transfusions to a sieve
 or something equally futile.
Yet I *knew* that there was *Something* . . . *Some Way* . . . *Some Answer.*
I'd better not wait *too long* to find out about it.
 I didn't have to wait that long.
 A series of Crises speeded up my Search.
 It became literally a *Fight for Life*
 as well as a *Search for Life.*
The Prodigal Son began finding his thoughts turning Homeward.
I searched the religions, faiths and cults of the world.
I read Yogi and ate Yogurt. I read psychology, psychiatry, psycho-
analysis, Dianetics, diarhettics, mental science, will power, occultism
and cultism. I gulped Physics, metaphysics and plain physics.
 I ended up with a fine case of Muddlephysics.
There was a Shining Thread running through All of this . . .
 but the Thread seemed to get lost in the garments.
 Intellectually I could grasp the ideas
 but there were too many ideas.

There would be glimpses and flashes
but they seemed to be Will-o'-the-Wisps,
and Ghost-Fires and Wraiths.
I needed an experience.
It came.
I began finding people with that look which I call Dynamic Serenity.
I talked with them . . . and *listened to them.* We exchanged ideas. I was
meeting Companion Vagabonds of the Joyous Journey to Joy-Age.
I was finding answers which I felt that I could pass-along to
the young G.I. who had said, "Sarge, what do you think about
this God Business?" *They were answers which worked for me.*

ONEHOOD

Far-scattered Brotherhood, we meet and pass,
    Flashing the Silent Signal with our eyes,
    Or wait the Sign like people, weather-wise,
Who read the clouds and shadows on the grass.
No Blatant Banners signify our Clan;
    We meet and walk a little way together,
    Talking of casual things, of times and weather,
Until a word or phrase arches the Span
Of Separateness. After that we go
    Our Solitary Roads, but not alone;
    We walk in Onehood, braving the Unknown
More valiantly than ever since we *know*
That we are One with star and grass and sun;
    Our Kinship lies beyond sheer Time and Space
    For in our Brother's face we see our Face,
And feel the mighty heart-throb of the One.

A Ponder-Over for the Journey.
    Nothing UNimportant ever happens to you.
    Nothing that you do is ever Unimportant.
    Knowing that . . . could you be bored?

The Second Atom Bomb was an apparently casual statement by Leo Keppler of Rhapsody Record Shop in Hollywood, California.

THIS IS THE STORY OF THE SECOND ATOM BOMB ON VAGABOND'S HOUSE

My Friend, with casual grace and cool aplomb,
Tossed me a verbal super-atom bomb.
It detonated with a quiet thunder
Leaving me dazed and palpitant with wonder.
　Atomic bombs, the usual sort, explode,
　Destroying worlds with powers that corrode
　And render toxic all the atmosphere,
　Leaving an aftermath of Death and Fear.
While super-atomic bombs destroy the Old
And Shop-Worn Worlds of Thought. Lo, and behold!
Quick to our hands are mounds of broken stone
To shape new structures such as our Hearts have known
In dreams. *Five simple words in line together*
Magicked to nothingness the old strong tether
Which bound my Heart, a slave to false desires
Which burned to ash in the New World's cleansing fires.
　"Joy is an inside job," he said. The phrase
　Circled within my mind. To my amaze
　I realized that it said something older,
　"Beauty is in the Eyes of the Beholder."
Of course! My mind had known it all the while,
But youth-wise took it with indulgent smile
As something used for mottoes, stale and trite . . .
Copy-book maxims for young hands to write.
　"Joy is an inside job." How strong and terse
　This streamlined modern statement of a verse

Which, like an old fine cloak worn gray and thin,
Yet warms, *"The Kingdom of Heaven is within."*
HEAVEN . . . the state of Heart that knows sure peace.
BEAUTY . . . the balm that gives the Heart surcease.
JOY . . . the artesian spring that ever flows
Beneath the earth-flesh from Eternal Snows.
And all within, *within* . . . Joy, Beauty, Heaven.
I had searched the years through seven times seven
And seven years more, in people, places, things,
For that which only the Inner Finding brings.
Hear the old clarion challenge newly throb
In streamlined idiom, *"Joy is an inside job."*

****** ****** ******

THE FEEL OF IT

Before we go on to the Third Atom Bomb you might logically say,
"Aren't you giving exaggerated importance to the mere statement
and wording of an idea in your Second Atom Bomb?"
I don't think so. The cold wind strikes the amorphous vapor of a
cloud precipitating it as rain, hail or snow. It's a case of timing.
In 1944 a crippling neuritis blocked my work as an artist and writer.
After months of futile searching for relief I reached my lowest low
one morning in the black hour of pre-dawn.
I had slept soddenly, toxic with exhaustion.
I awakened with every nerve alerted.
Thoughts were coming in but I wasn't thinking them consciously.
A Silent Partner was *wordlessly* releasing thoughts into my mind.
"Everyone in this world is shaped for a work
which is essentially his or hers . . . for a purpose.
We don't choose our talents. They choose us.
You have humanly and selfishly served yourself. Now, and at long last
you will serve your Veritable Self. For that you were formed and made.
Rebel and you will be prisoner of your pain.
Acquiesce and you will be guided surely."
Can you remember this in the morning? *Who spoke to whom and who
heard?*

→

One, two, three, four, five, six, seven, eight, nine, ten, eleven and twelve events followed; twelve decisions and actions were taken which were so fantastically opposed to common sense (which is so common because there's actually so little sense in it) and so right in the light of what I know now that to relate them would put me into the realm of Science Fiction. Three . . . *coincidence.* Twelve . . . *no.*

The right line in the right paragraph on the right page
of the right book at the right time for right action.
Opening the right door at the right time to meet the right
person at the right place for the right move . . . etc.

This included the inspired eeny-meeny-miney-mo choice of Dr. Raymond Whalley of Hollywood who was the only one who could . . . or *did* put me medically over the physical hump until I could again follow the thread which had been put into my hand . . . and into my heart.

I knew that a miracle had happened but, like the accidental
solving of a puzzle, I didn't know how it had come about.

I read over three hundred books on spiritual and mental healing.
A line here, a clue there; a cloud of ideas, but as yet amorphous.
Ernest Holmes once challenged me, *"What do you mean by amorphous."*

I told him, *"A squashed morph."* My mental state was *just that.*
Advertising Experts are given high salaries for the right "name."
Contests with large prizes are offered for a "selling slogan."

A phrase will sometimes nozzle the undirected energies
of a great nation into one powerful irresistible stream.

A singing coach once said, "You're singing *notes.* Get the *feel* of it."
I was singing the notes of my new-found discovery but I had lost the
"feel of it." I had lost that *certainty* which brought me through crisis.
I still thought that the miracle was something that I myself had done.

I was floundering in the world of will-power, up-and-at-'em,
the I-Ego, John Ego Adamsmith's cocky world, the Willful Will.
I had heard the words "Kingdom of Heaven" all during my youth-days.
But I couldn't get the "feel" of it.

Due to my lack of perception of the symbolism I had accepted, or rather, had rejected the white nighties, amateur harp players and the Streets on the Gold Standard of early teachings. Heaven was hooey.

Please turn to page 142

[28]

I DIED AT DAWN

An "X" drawn with invisible disappearing ink
on the vast indifferent surface of the blue Pacific
somewhere between Agana, Guam, Marianas Islands,
and Majuro, Marshall Islands, marks the spot
  where I died at dawn.
Sometimes I feel that it is my happy ghost telling this story.
  We expect great crises in our lives to have bells ringing,
perhaps lightning, burning bushes and other spectacles.
  Often they happen so quietly.
An Observer would have seen only a Man standing at the ship's rail,
watching the phenomenon of Dawn, a super-spectacle in Technicolor.
Only a betraying weary sag of the shoulders and a stilled tense-
ness of listening would have revealed the signs of Crisis.
  Every sense seemed to be tuned to a Hopeless Expectancy.
  Expectancy of what?   The Man could not know.
It is my belief that an Immaterial but Real Presence, which I call
Silent Partner, *guides us when we accept its Guidance to the exact*
spot in Time-Space where the missing pieces of our Perfect Pattern
await our recognition and acceptance . . . and use. This conviction did
not crystallize until this related experience was complete.
  Four things I have always loathed and avoided when possible:
very hot humid weather, the limited space of a ship at sea,
  the claustrophobia of cramped quarters . . . and *aloneness.*
I have long known the Aloneness-among-Crowds. There one may throw
out the casual line of conversation and snag a guppy of transient com-
panionship, to ease the ache of Loneliness.
  Why then did I go to the Prickly Heat Paradise of Micronesia;
why spend months on a freighter in the blue vastnesses of sea
with a Captain-companion who spent half of his time withdrawn
into the Polaris aloneness of his moods when the Sea lays its
finger of Silence on the Lips of Men of the Sea?
Why then did I sleep in a six-by-ten cabin with only the unsatisfying
company of myself, the ship's cockroaches and a native crew who
spoke mostly glug-glugese?

Why then did I go to an experience where I experienced such Alone-ness-with-Aloneness as I have never known, astringent and corrosive? Because there, stripped of the many diversions and expediencies for avoiding thinking which are available to us in our States-side World, I had to face a question. The Answer was the Third Atom Bomb.

I DIED AT DAWN

At dawn I looked with jaundiced eye
On sea and cloud and sun and sky.
   The clouds were merely senseless vapor
   Piled up like heaps of tissue paper.
The vast, indifferent, endless sea
Stretched on beyond Infinity.
   The sky which should have been sublime
   Was far . . . impersonal as Time.
   The voices in the wind that cried
   Were my own sorrows amplified
   In syllables of nameless pain
   Blown back into my heart again.
The sun, that friendly yellow disc,
Was just a flaming asterisk
Upon a page of chilly blue.
This was not the sky I knew.
   The far horizons made a cell
   Imprisoning, a wall-less Hell
   Where curse or prayer or cry would be
   Articulate futility.
Far better in despair to try
To paste a stamp upon the sky.
   No little gesture would suffice,
   No wheedling, no trick device,

No bribe, evasion, platitude
Would serve. I stood there, starkly nude,
Flayed of my hide, my empty ME,
Stripped of its self-sufficiency,
Drained of its arrogance and pride
With nought without and nought inside.
  No thing in all the world was less
  Than I . . . a point of consciousness
  Yet conscious only of the ache
  Of formless chains I could not break . . .
  No words to speak, no gestures willed.
  I died within . . . my Self was stilled,
  No pulses stirred, no fevered breath:
  At last I knew . . . "This . . . this is Death."
As acquiescent as the rain
That falls into the sea again
I felt myself dissolve in space.
And then . . . I saw the faceless Face
And heard the voiceless Voice. I knew
Beyond all knowing . . . this is true . . .
  "God is. God *is.* And *All is God.*
  The sea, the sky, the cloud, the clod,
  And you and I and star and sun
  And time and space in God *are One."*
Never again will I make moan
That I am lonely or alone.
  The dawn became one flaming bliss.
  My newborn heart saw Genesis.

Nothing changed, yet everything changed . . . from Simple Conscious-
ness to Self-Consciousness to Cosmic or Veritable Consciousness. Then
. . . the Prodigal returns to Babylon; the world-pictures, viewed
through the limited betraying senses, blur and clear like home movies.
But the Great Voice echoes and re-echoes with the Seventh Statement . . . *"God saw everything that he had made, and behold . . . it was*
very good."

AND THEN WHAT?

This is going to be difficult to tell.
It smacks of a synthetic saint with a Neon halo and a white nightie
being interviewed at a masquerade party by columnist Hedda Hay-
hopper.

Yet now I can see that the inevitable natural progression
from Simple Consciousness or *Lily-and-Fido Consciousness*
to Self Consciousness or *John Ego Adamsmith Consciousness*
to Veritable or Cosmic Consciousness (*God Consciousness*)
is as sure and beautiful as the emergence of the ripened seed
from the enveloping fruit from the fulfilled flower from the
adolescent bud from the proffering stem from the supporting
trunk from the nourishing roots from the releasing seed.
In the eternal cycling of life from Source and back to Source *only form
changes;* the impulse is one progression or emergence.

"My newborn heart *saw* Genesis." An insight which before
had been flickeringly and partially with me became vividly,
for a moment which might have been an hour, a clarity of vision
which has never wholly departed. The vision was non-visual.
I saw the "Pattern-as-Perfect" *within* and *without; cosmic.*

Heretofore Genesis with its statement *"saw that it was very good"*
was so obviously wrong . . . as viewed through the astigmatic eyes of
John Ego Adamsmith.

*At one moment the whole world was "out of step" except me.
My focus-of-awareness shifted (I do not know how nor why)
and suddenly that which had been mockingly meaningless and cruel
and indifferent in the Universe became splendid and flawless.*
I could almost hear the great smooth machinery
of the Universe moving in absolute synchronization. I saw
the transiency of John Ego Adamsmith's world of senses
and intellect, and the eternality of the Veritable World
which Jesus, Paul and other great mystics of all time had
tried to reveal to us. It was not a progressive realization.
It was instantaneous and without volition. There was no
sense of *"I";* only realization of *"am"* . . . of *being.*

It was as though a plastic skin sloughed off, giving my whole being a larger breathing.

It was as though the lens of my eyes suddenly achieved telescopic, microscopic and X-ray vision.

It was not an intellectual realization . . . I have never had headaches from too much intellect.

God knows (*and that's just what I mean*) it was no reward for virtue.

It was an inner seeing and an inner knowing;

yet no emotion in my whole life was so intense.

I can not prove this to you.

You can not disprove it for me.

My experience was no more unique than the sprouting of a seed.

It was only individual.

There was nothing supernatural about it.

It was so supremely natural that I wondered how I could have gone a half century *without* this clarification.

"Evil" is in man's human attitude, his misunderstanding.

"Sin" and "Evil" are simply the wrong method. "Sin" is "missing the mark," "losing balance and falling." "Suffering" is not punishment, but rather the inevitable reaction from wrong or faulty action.

The Road-Signs and Patrin *are everywhere about us for us to see.* Jesus gave the flawless Road-Maps and showed the Perfect Pattern. Why do we not see *until we see?* Hundreds of volumes have been written on the subject. Perhaps the answers are in the volumes.

But books *about* water are *not water. They do not quench thirst.* Thirst is quenched by the *"experience of water."* Veritable Self is known by the *"experience of Veritable Consciousness."*

Personal Self, which I call John Ego Adamsmith, or in moments of exasperation, Romeo Lancelot Hamm, is like a costume and theatrical make-up, or a skin which peels off after sunburn. It is superimposed upon the Veritable Self which is nameless yet more real than the flesh and muscles which are at this moment moving this typewriter to action.

Veritable self is not a separate entity, not a part-apart.

How and why did this happen? I do not know.

Perhaps, in the vastness and silence of the great sea-spaces and my aloneness-with-aloneness, I learned to "be still and listen" and in that stillness to *hear* and to *know*.

I was so weary of my petty Personal Self that if I could have taken it off like a sweaty shirt I would have thrown it into the sea so willingly and regretlessly. Most of the time *now* I am aware that my Personal or Seeming-Self IS a garment; it is a Public Relations Self or Contact Man for dealing with the world of tangibles.

This freedom from Personal Self is intermittent because of habit reflexes. Old gestures and mannerisms cling persistently, but it is *persistence,* also, which finally eliminates them.

The World of Appearances, far from becoming vague, became more vividly and colorfully joy-filled than ever before, recognized as the Realm of Effect but not the Realm of Cause. "Cause" is the Veritable Consciousness. See "Then you Know," page 159.

The Dynamic Idea which makes a flower to become a flower seems to say: *"Don't look only at color and form.* See ME, the Living Creative Idea *speaking in color and form to* the *Living Idea of You* in *flesh, mind* and *spirit."*

I realized that I was not a semi-conscious puppet, looking AT Life, and seeing, tasting, touching and hearing Life.

In my Veritable Self I *AM* Life.

Just as You, in your Veritable Self, *are* Life.

We are in no wise separate in our Veritable Selves.

     We *are* Time.

     We *are* Life.

     We *are* Joy.

But only as we consciously express these ideas can we en-joy them or live in-joy-of-them, emergent from Veritable or God-Consciousness.

Love, which had been adhesive and possessive, clutching and killing that which it clutched, became *non-personal,* which is quite different from *impersonal.*

Because there is no desire to *possess,* there is no fear of *losing.*

We live in anticipation of life, not in dread of death.

→

An architect cleared a point for me which may have helped in realization. A client complained that his house was sagging, the roof leaking and the plumbing plugged. The architect proved that the blueprint was perfect and the specifications adapted to make a worthy house. BUT *the Contractor had used shoddy materials, substituting cheaper and inferior construction.* There it is, The Pattern is perfect, but we, humanly, are constantly substituting our limited ideas for the ideas of Creative God . . . and the House-of-our-Life sags, the roof leaks, the plumbing plugs.

John Ego Adamsmith, in his ignorance, ignores the specifications and blueprints which are his heritage. He *evicts himself* from Eden.

*** *** *** *** ***

The Senses, which had been riders with spurs, roweling my flanks until they bled, became what they should be, horses for me to ride on the Joyous Journey.

I realized that Joy is a direct artesian out-flow of God-Consciousness.

This Joy heals
as a fresh wind *heals* the stuffiness of a closed room when
the windows are opened.

This Joy heals
as the light *heals* the darkness of an unlighted room.

Joy is truly the pulse of God, since it is the inarticulate vitalizing realization that Life *is* eternal, immortal and constantly renewed as the experience of the One Consciousness, God, emerging from its inseparable Oneness into Individual Awareness.

Only later and very slowly did these realizations crystallize until I could shape them, awkwardly and inadequately as you can see, as thoughts in words to pass-along to you in case that you can use them.

The great Patrin of our Greatest Guide, Jesus with Christ-consciousness, change from *printed words* to *cosmic gongs,* vibrating their meaning to our inner understanding. They no longer need explanation; *they need to be lived.*

WHAT AM I TRYING TO PROVE?

Now, Companion-Vagabond, you might ask, *"What are you trying to prove?"*

The answer is, *"N O T H I N G."*

Nothing is more futile than trying to prove verbally that which is its own proof yet which must be proven through direct experience.

The Power of the Presence of Creative God-Consciousness *in our* lives and *as our lives* is its own proof, *irrefutable.*

But, in our Realization, Recognition and Trust in the Power of The Presence lies our Joy, our Health, our Security and our Release from the Tyranny of Fear. Is it practical? Is gravity practical?

This is not, *as claimed by many,* a misty, musty *Flight from Reality* indulged in by "sentimental, superstitious frustrated females and womanish males."

It is a Journey TO Reality, and some of our pioneer guides are the top-flight (and I mean TOP-flight) scientists, astronomers, physicists, psychologists, leaders of progressive industry as well as our spiritual and metaphysical seekers and searchers. *Read Margaret Lee Runbeck's ANSWER WITHOUT CEASING for some of those names and stories.*

We American people have gambled heavily on our truly incredible Mechanical Age to bring security, happiness, health, speed, comfort and power. We can teach a boy to drive a car but *until we can teach him to drive himself, he is a potential menace to Life.*

Until we learn to use our Spiritual Power to guide us in the use of our Mechanical and Atomic Power we will *misuse* it. Our supersonic speed will speed us more swiftly to destruction; for one Wing of Mercy we will have a hundred Wings of Death. The proof is before our eyes today, as we cower in the demoniac light of H-bombs.

Our cynical and materialistic writers, brilliant, cocksure and convincing, have dominated our viewpoint. The shrillness of their whistling now betrays their fear of the dark which they have spread among us. *Their fear becomes our fear.*

In twenty-five years of lecturing on the Three-Way-Stretch-Girdle-Gobble-and-Gabble Circuit I have seen the betraying look of Spiritual Malnutrition on the face of America . . . and on my own face.

It is the look of a man haunted by an *invisible* ghost.

Magazines are increasingly punctuated with articles on Nervous Tension, How to Be Happy in Twelve Easy Lessons Without Effort, How to Influence People and Get Yourself Thoroughly Detested, etc., etc.

Our A-Bombs and H-Bombs and X-Y-Z-Bombs are *not* protecting us when the enemy can reply with Q-Bombs, P.D.Q.-Bombs and ZYX-Bombs. Air-conditioning does not cure Heart-Conditioning. Switches can turn on every kind of light but Inner Light. Supersonic speed only moves us, *with our anxieties and neuroses,* from one place to another faster.

Neither in the Stratosphere nor the Bathysphere did we find The Promised Land or the Kingdom of Heaven or *"any reasonable facsimile of same."*

As I said, I know the futility of trying to prove anything verbally. But I can testify happily that with the deep realization that in the *Power of the Presence of God-Consciousness,* not as a remote and distant thing to be plead for, but as an *immediate and ever-present power,* awaiting only recognition and acceptance, lies the Land of Joy-Age or the Kingdom of Heaven, or the Peace of Heart which is beyond any other treasure, tangible or intangible, in the world.

Now the words Soul, Spirit, Christ, God, Lord and others which I had detoured because of unacceptable associations and connotations have become *words of Power.* For a long time those words were archaic; they carried the association of something distant, of another age, of inaccessibility, along with the odors of un-sanctity which came from their misuse by demagogues, fanatics, charlatans and spiritual dilettantes.

Dissolve these encrustations; then truly our hands are filled, not only with pearls of great price, but with instruments for making a new world for ourselves, a new life and a newly discovered Self that it is a Joy to live with . . . and in.

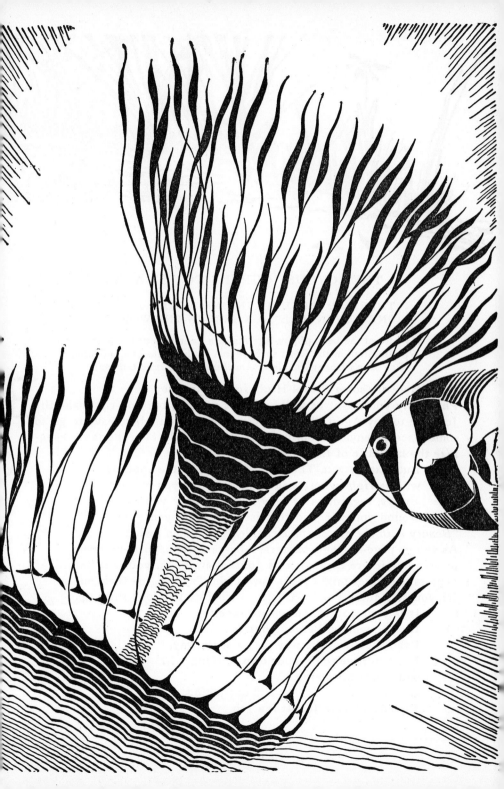

THE JOYOUS JOURNEY TO JOY-AGE

THREE ADVENTURES IN ONE WORLD or
ONE ADVENTURE IN THREE-IN-ONE-WORLD.

My Idea of the Land of Joy-Age May Be Your Idea of the Last
Whistle-Stop on the Road to Boredom in the State of Confusion.
One Man's Honey-Suckle Is Another Man's Skunk-Cabbage.

Here are some Travel-Hints for the Journey.
Physically you might be a Shut-In for a while, but you can make the
Journey to Joy-Age right where you are. Or you might have to go to
some place as remote as Majuro, Marshall Islands, Micronesia to *recognize* the last Mile of the Journey.

But, I warn you, The Last Mile-End of the Journey
will be *right where you started,* where *you are
always,* regardless of how much scenery you move
around yourself, and that is . . . *within yourself.*
"Beauty is in the eye of the Beholder." Joy is an inside job.
As you go page-by-page, paragraph-by-paragraph, poem-by-poem,
picture-by-picture through this Journey-by-Book, you will find
expressions which might seem new or odd. Try to figure them out
for yourself, these Ponder-Overs . . . before you look them up.

It is *your* Joy which we are seeking.
It's you who will enjoy *your* Joy.
I can show you the way . . . a little way.
But you have to do your own walking . . .
and your own seeing . . .
and your own in-joying and out-joying.
Joy IS an inside Job. It *is* a Job.

WHAT IS JOY?

"Just what is Joy?" you ask. I can't explain
What happens when the dry earth feels the rain
But there is a swift response within the seed
That stirs to verdant life to meet a need
For fruitful growth, an ardent quickening.
The seed depends on sun and rain and spring
To give the signal for the glad release
Of still potential power. The caprice
Of weather, like a tyrant's whim, withholds
Or gives the royal order that unfolds
The prisoned plant. My heart, *that curious seed,*
Holds magic *within itself* to meet its need.
 My thoughts are rain-gods, summoning from thin air
 The blessed rain, the sunlight warm and fair
 To stir the earth-flesh into fertile power
 And lure the vine of joy to radiant flower.

Joy is the heart-search going bravely forth
To follow the wild goose trumpets, sounding North.
 Joy is response to life, the urge to song
 That swells the linnet's throat; *Joy* is the gong
 Of dawn resounding in the hearts of men
 After a vigiled night. *Joy* is the wren
 That feels the eggs astir beneath her breast.
 Joy is the glad expectancy, the zest
 Of living in Youth's clear, far-searching eyes.
 Joy is the pilot winging down free skies
 To distant goals. *Joy* is the flooding light
 That banishes dark specters of the night.
"Just what is Joy?" you ask. Turn to the clod
Within your breast . . . *Joy is the pulse of God.*

Silent Partner says, "When you were thirty your heart had beat roughly (some-times very roughly) one billion and one hundred million times. Did you make your heart? Could you make it beat? Is it not truly "the pulse of God?" Is each of the millions of hearts in the world its own self-sustaining power plant, or is there One Power pulsing in all?

BIRDS OF AN ODD FEATHER FLOCK TOGETHER

Some odd birds of odd plumage will flock together on this Journey.

SILENT PARTNER. He's an old friend. You'll meet him often. He is the voice of your Veritable Self, speaking through intuition and using some curious mouthpieces.

JOHN EGO ADAMSMITH and JANE EGO EVESMITH. They're US. *Adam, Eve* . . . for race. *Smith* for family. *John, Jane,* for individual. And *Ego* for personality. We are legion. With our focus-of-awareness in the senses and the intellect we look on a world where people die, friendships fail, fortunes crash, cyclones and atomic bombs destroy homes, fine people seem to have the toughest luck, while rat people and cockroach people seem to thrive.

ROMEO LANCELOT HAMM. The Devil, if there ever was a Devil. The Ego rampant. Such an engaging, persuasive devil, so convincing, so plausible, such a salesman (for his own ends), and as undependable as a tissue-paper umbrella in a rainstorm. He's one of those areas-of-our-awareness which acts almost like a person.

There shouldn't be a dull moment with that Gang along.

**** **** **** ****

The Impulse to Express Joy . . . is as natural as the impulse to walk, to talk, to grow and to live. *Joy is one of the dynamics of living*.

Nothing can make us joyful. We *are* joy-filled. We *are* Joy.

Joy is the natural emanation of the Veritable Self,

as radio-activity is the natural radiation of uranium.

NEITHER THE CORK NOR THE CORKSCREW makes the jug to be full of water, of milk or molasses or cider. The jug is already cider-full, water-full, milk-full or molasses-full. Just as we are joy-full.

THE COMBINATION OF CORKSCREW, cork and a strong powerful pull *induces*

or makes the way ready for the artesian outflow.

We learn to uncork ourselves, let joy be literally *unconfined*.

Do not say, "I feel joyful."

Say and think, rather, "I AM JOY . . . expressing."

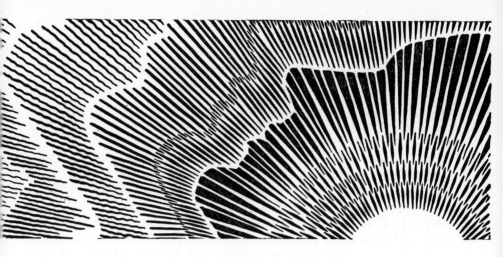

IDIOM OF JOY-AGE

Since we are talking of Joy, seeking Joy and journeying to the Land of Joy-Age, let us try to understand Joy in the Idiom of Joy-Age . . .

For me . . .

The *word* "Joy" is dynamic . . . self-starter for Joy itself.

The *word* "Joy" is radio-active with zest and energy.

The *word* "Joy" has the vitality and promise of delight
like the popping of a champagne cork for revelers.

The *word* "Joy" is the corkscrew for uncorking the bottle
of sparkling waters . . . but *Joy itself* is the effervescence released.

The *word* "Joy" is the match to the sky-climbing rocket of
delight . . . but *Joy itself* is the propelling power within the rocket.

The *word* "Joy" is the command, *"Forward! March!"* to the
Soldiers of our Inner Strengths. Speak it with authority.

The *word* "Joy" is more an exclamation of radiant happiness
than the name of a thing, tangible or intangible.

The *word* "Joy" is the Open-Sesame to Treasures of Happiness.

The *word* "Joy" is a syllable of laughter.	Joy.
The *word* "Joy" is a Talisman.	Joy.
"Joy" itself is artesian.	Joy.
"Joy" is inexhaustible.	Joy.
"Joy" is within.	Joy.
Release it.	Joy.
JOY!	JOY.

P.S. Why is this splendid definition of Joy obsolete? "Praise in Thanksgiving."
Joy *is* the inarticulate emotion of *thanks beyond words* for inner delight, for
well-being and being well.

ROAD-MAPS, SIGN-POSTS, PATRIN* and
THINGS LIKE THAT

Patrin or Patteran, in Gypsy Talk, a handful of leaves, twigs, and grasses ar-
ranged in certain designs and laid by the Roadside or at the Fork-of-the-Road
indicating to those who follow and can read the signs, "We went this way."

ROAD-SIGN PATRIN. If I offered you the choice between $1 and $10
and $100 you'd take the $100 because the $100 includes the $10 and the $1.

If you choose JOY you have Pleasure and Happiness included.

We are looking for answers to the $100 question.

PATRIN. It is known that a Man guides by two dictionaries. One, the
meanings in the book. Two, his private and personal interpretations due
to reactions, connotations, prejudices and preferences formed consciously or unconsciously during living.

For instance. The dictionary says that Spinach is a "pot-herb of
the Middle East cultivated for its edible leaves.   HA!

My private dictionary says, "Spinach, *a loathsome mess, cooked with-*
out inspiration, served without enthusiasm and eaten without relish.
I hope someday to eat it without *prejudice.*

In order for us to understand each other we must speak in the Idiom
of Joy-Age, the Slang of the Road, and be able to read the Patrin.

Idiom of Joy-Age is not just what the words mean but what we mean by
our use of the words. Like youngsters' Pig-Latin, it's *between us.*

Should we let a dictionary dictate to us?

The Journey to Joy-Age is Three Adventures in One World, but also
One Adventure in a Three-in-One-World, Physical, Mental, Spiritual.

PHYSICAL ADVENTURE, Sensuous Images, Pleasures, Sights, Hard-
ships and Delights with Senses for *Guide* . . . don't let them take over.

MENTAL ADVENTURE, Psychological Twists of the Road, Hazards, Excitements, with Lively Curiosity for Guide. (John Ego Adamsmith . . . not Romeo Lancelot Hamm.) Let him *point out* but not *dictate* the way.

SPIRITUAL ADVENTURE or Awareness of the Immaterial but Real
World of Cause behind the appearances. The Veritable Self is Censor of
the Tall Tales that our guides, John Ego Adamsmith and Romeo Lancelot Hamm try to "sell us" and "tell us."

Whatever your Age, your Joy-Age is Now . . . when you realize it.

SONS OF DUST

I know that Seed of the Tumbleweed
  Fell in my heart when I was young,
  For I am an alien Weed among
The constant plants of the Rooted Breed,
For often and ever I know the need
  Of Chance and Change, the Siren View
  Beyond the Hill, the Strange, the New.
Going and blowing at driven speed,
Frail of will as the bending reed
  When Winds of Wanderlust pipe their flutes
  And Gypsy Rhythms loosen the roots.
The roots are shallow, the soil is need
Of Change for Seeds of the Tumbleweed.
  The World is wide and the Sea is deep,
  And where I wander and where I sleep
Is little worry, since Life is short
At its longest span for the Restless Sort.
  Go I *would* and go I *must*,
  Seed of the Tumbleweed . . . Son of Dust.

*The Restlessness of the Tumbleweed Heart is the Divine Claustrophobia urging
the Seeker toward Released Horizons.*
*The Veritable Self, being one with Life, is scornful of all fences, adhesion-proof
and too flexible for shackles. It is joyously free.*

TIPS FOR COMPANION-VAGABONDS
on THE JOYOUS JOURNEY TO JOY-AGE

As a Companion-Vagabond acting as Informal Guide on this
Joyous Journey, I suggest . . .
Take your time. . . . We *are* Time . . . so we have all the time in the
world.

Because it's not so much how far you go
As how much you see.
It's not so much how much you see
As how much you learn
From what you see.
It's not so much how much you learn
As how much you do
With what you learn
From what you see
As you go
Wherever you are trying
To go.

A PONDER-OVER FOR THE JOURNEY

Silent Partner told me, "You have loved adhesively.
Fear of aloneness was the mucilage of adhesion.
You were like one who is drowning
who drowns his rescuer through fear of drowning.
    Hold your hands *open* in the sunlight.
    They are filled with light.
Try to hold that sunlight by closing your hands upon it.
You hold shadows, darkness, aloneness.
    Joy is released from within.
Those who seek Joy in exterior things
are the Vacuum-Cleaner people,
sucking in the dry dusts of perishable moments.
Those who release Joy from within
are the Lawn Sprinkler people,
outflowing from inexhaustible artesian wells of Joy
within,
Refreshing and refreshed.

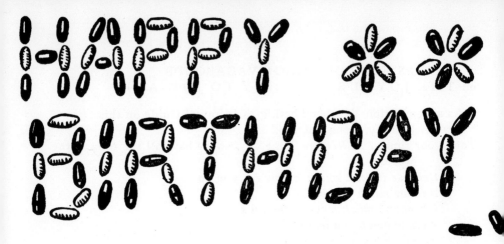

In my half-century of living I have attended some beautiful birthday parties, and have had a few of my own which were memorable. The most spectacular one was given by Princes Abigail Kawananakoa of Hawaii, when two thousand guests were proffered a luau so sumptuous, so regal in the Polynesian manner that only the hardiest survived the plethora of delights.

Army barracks in the dead of winter at Fort Ontario, N.Y., at that time of the month when Pay Day was only a distant hope, and cash was as scarce as red-flannels on the Island of Yap . . . that was the setting for the most beautiful birthday party I ever attended. This is the true story of it.

PRIVATE WILLIE'S BIRTHDAY PARTY

His name was William (Brown or Smith or Jones,
I don't recall) . . . one of the vast unknowns,
The cover-crop plowed under without fame
To make our Nation's history . . . or its shame.
    I don't know why we didn't call him "Bill"
    Or "William" or even simply homely "Will."
    For reasons, soldier-wise, we chose the silly
    Yet strangely fitting nickname "Private Willie"
    To label that big frame, man-statured, yet boy-hearted,
    During our brief war-comradeship, soon parted,
    That bound us in a friendliness that filled
    The aching need of love when crisis chilled
    And frosted all the slower blooms of life.
    No time for deeper rootage when the knife

Threatens the bud.
                    When welcome "Mail Call" came
Each soldier waited tensely for his name,
"*Zybowski . . . Perkins . . . Van de Veer . . . McKim.*"
It meant that somewhere someone thought of him.
      Each soldier on his bunk explored each word
      For hidden meaning, as a hungry bird
      Searches the soil for seeds and scattered grain . . .
      Those letters bringing joy or sudden pain
      Packaged in words, sweet, polished or uncouth,
      "*Hey, Fellers, look! My kid's got his first tooth!*"
Or, in a voice that pain made dark and hoarse,
"*Whaddya know, my wife wants a divorce.*"
      Outside the circle Private Willie lingered,
      His name uncalled. We who fondly fingered
      Letters and pictures failed to realize
      At first the stark long hunger in his eyes,
      The look of a lost pup, hoping without hope
      For the friendly pat, the word, or even the rope
      Of loving bondage. Birthdays brought our gang
      Presents of socks or books or the homey tang
Of cookies, shared and munched . . . sometimes a cake
Inch-deep with frosting such as "mothers love to make."
He shared the news of *our* families, tears or jokes,
But never a word we heard of his own folks.
      Private Willie, hesitant at first,
      Soon learned to share with a pride that almost burst
      The buttons from his shirt when a buddy cried
      The old-new boast of fatherhood. He sighed
      With the lovelorn in *their* sighings, and he kept
      Secrets of muttered talk when soldiers slept.

We loved this homely, pug-nosed freckled kid
And did those awkward things that shyly hid
Our sympathy and helplessness to heal

The deep hurt loneliness that eyes reveal
In quick unguarded moments. One gray day
When Pay Day seemed a thousand years away
And cash was slim and cigarettes were few,
The Sergeant told us something that he knew,
    "That kid ain't never got a single card
    Or letter since he's here. He takes it hard
    Inside. His nineteenth birthday is today.
    You want to throw a party? Whaddya say?
    Don't let him know. Keep it a big surprise.
    (Who would have dreamed *that* look in a Sergeant's eyes?)
    I'll see he's not around until it's time.
    O.K., get going. Here's a buck and a lousy dime.
    It's all I've got." The word was quickly passed,
    And from foot-lockers' depths were soon amassed
    Those treasures . . . small themselves, so great in giving,
    That come from the days of a soldier's meager living.
A tube of toothpaste (only *partly* squeezed),
Shaving soap, a harmonica that wheezed
A few bum squawks, but added a festive note,
An ashtray in the form of a rowdy goat,
A handkerchief (with the wrong initials on it),
A penciled birthday verse . . . *far from a sonnet,*
But rhymed in friendliness; *part* of a carton
Of smokes, a P-X cake with a candy heart on,
And one lone candle (God knows whence *it* came)
And a string of jelly-beans to spell the name
And message: "Happy Birthday, Private Willie."
It certainly wasn't elegant or frilly
But in those barren barracks the candle's light
Brought something luminous into the winter's night.

We heard his footsteps. *"Psst! Get set. He's coming."*
He froze in the door and stared. We started humming,

"Happy Birthday to you . . .
Happy Birthday to you . . .
Happy Birthday, Private Willie . . .
Happy Birthday to you-u-u-u-u. . . ."

Some things you just can't tell. That freckled face
Went blank, then twisted in a slow grimace
Of pain, so sweet and deep, that we could hear
Almost the trickle of the big round tear
That welled and spilled and faltered down his nose,
Easing the spell. Our raffish shouting rose,
"Happy Birthday, you so-and-so. Speech! Speech!"
Slowly his misted eyes searched deep in each
Of our buddy-eyes. His Adam's apple bobbed
In agony. *"You god-durned fools!"* he laughed and sobbed.
And we laughed too . . . and gulped. In happy daze
He opened one by one the gift displays,
Folding the papers, saying, *"Gosh, that's swell.*
Thank you, Fellers. I don't know how to tell . . ."
The words blurred out. A mighty raucous shout
Shook the bare barracks, and until "Lights out"
We sang . . . not good, but loud and long and hearty,
Sharing in Private Willie's birthday party.

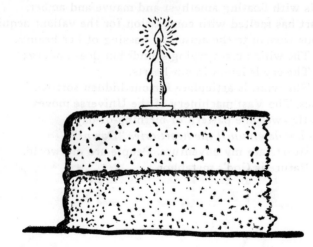

PEOPLE ARE MY WORLD

After half a century of world travel
I find that scenery is most beautiful
When it is background for a friendly face.

NATURE IS GOD'S METAPHOR

I have seen dawns at sea as glorious as Genesis in Technicolor,
And yet, for me, less beautiful than the flooding light of warmth
In welcoming eyes.
I have seen lagoons, serene and blue as celestial sapphires,
Less dreamily lovely than the tranquillity on the face
Of a woman happily in love.

>   I have *stood* in awe before great peaks
>   That thrust against the sky
>   In white defiance of the raging storms.
>   But I have *bowed* in awe
>   Before the high stark peaks of integrity
>   In hearts of men and women under crisis . . .
>   Not heroes only, but the little-great,
>   The humble-mighty of our daily living.

I have dissolved in the gentle melancholy of Indian summer
Veiling hills with floating amethyst and mauve and amber,
But my heart has melted with compassion for the valiant acquiescence
Of a gracious woman to the autumnal passing of her beauty.

>   The wind makes crying sounds but does not cry;
>   The cry is latent in our hearts.
>   The wind is articulate for our hidden sorrow.

The sun rises. The Vast machinery of the Universe moves
In its majestic awesome pattern of birthing-of-day.
But dawn is not dawn until the heart cries "Dawn!"

>   Hearts are my adventure. People are my world.
>   Nature is God's metaphor.

WHAT WOULD YOU TELL HIM NOW?

Companion Vagabond, you might ask me this question, "What would you tell the young G.I. *now* if he were to ask you today, 'What do you think of this God Business, Sarge?'"
I think that I would tell him this story . . .

BARK, BRAVE PUP

A Very Small Dog was being put out into a Very Large Dark Night.
His Barking-End was very brave. His Wagging-End betrayed him.
           He was scared.
"The Bears are So BIG and My Bark is so small"
His Master understood.
"If all you little dogs," he said, "would bark together you would
make such a Terrible Thunder that it would scare the Biggest Grizzly
Bear in the World. Bark, Brave Pup."

I think that I would tell the young G.I. . . . .
    "This is not a time of Great Prophets.
    The Mighty Voices spoke.
    Their Reverberant Thunder still echoes through the Universe.
    But Man's Clamorous Insistencies, his Puny Querulousness,
    His Shrill Vindictiveness and his Braggart Boastings have drowned
    the Mighty Thunders, or dulled the ears that should hear.
    This is the Time for Many Small Voices Lifted in Unison.
    Add your Voice. *Bark, Brave Pup.*"

This young G.I. whose name I do not remember but whose face I shall
never forget, asked a simple question . . . such a terribly simple question that it turned my life upside down in a geologic shift of human
values of such magnitude (to me) that I am still trying to get acclimated
and oriented.

We do not know what our small bark may do to specters of the night
and the ghosts of the darkness. That is why I lift my small bark . . . to
pay a debt and to keep a promise.

I might even get you to barking.

I think that I would say this: "Bucko, let's take time off to talk.
    Let's talk . . . and talk . . . and talk
    until there isn't any talk left in us.
    Then let's quit talking
    and do some thinking.
    Then let's quit thinking,
    or what we *think* is *thinking*,
    and do some *realizing*.
    Maybe we'll get somewhere."
Then I'd try to do the impossible
which is to tell him what I feel and know, but can't explain,
so that he could feel and know.
    Nothing that I could tell him
    about what I feel and know
    would explain to him what I feel and know,
But, while I'm talking and while he's listening
we *might,* between us, open a shutter of his mind
so that *his own feeling and knowing*
would come through to his conscious realization.
Because in his Veritable Self *he does feel and know,*
just as you, in your Veritable Consciousness,
feel and know the answers.
But we never know just what is going to open that shutter.
That's why we search and read and listen and seek and seek some more.
    We're looking for whatever it is that *triggers that shutter.*
    The answers will come from within.

***   ***   ***

Because each Mind has its own Thought-Soil in which it flourishes best, I think I'd show him my book-shelves and say, "Browse there."

If he had the scientific slant he'd find Millikan, Toynbee, Eddington, Steinmetz, Jung, de Noüy, Jeans and many others speaking from their own slant.

He could take "The Universe and Dr. Einstein" by Lincoln Barnett

Continued on page 124

When I knew very little
I knew that I knew it all;
Now that I know a very little more
I know that I know nothing.
Perhaps, at long last, I know something.

IF THIS BE ALL . . .

If breeding, feeding,
Trying, crying,
Being born,
Harshly torn
From tortured flesh
To start afresh
Breeding, feeding,
Trying, crying,
Dying . . .
  If this be all
  It is not worth the climb,
  The fall.
But *there is more,*
Some near-far shore,
Some white high peak
To seek.
  This we know,
  So,
  We can go
  Trying, crying,
  Beyond dying
Seeking always,
All ways . . .
Hearing the clear long Call . . .
The Search is all.

Silent Partner says, "Ultimately we learn that we do not start the Search until we have found that for which we are seeking. The Search ends when we *realize* that we have taken with us, all the way, that which we sought . . . our Veritable Selves.

COMPANION VAGABONDS

For me . . . We are Companion Vagabonds because we are all individual *extensions-of-consciousness* of the *One Creative Consciousness, God,* experiencing itself through form and activity.

We are in no way separate except as we are aware, through the five limited and fallible senses, of multiplicity of form and variety of activity and purpose. But this is an *illusion* of *separateness.*

The One Creative Consciousness, the One Creative Power, the One Creative Presence is aware of itself in oneness but experiences itself in form and activity *as* every created thing, including Man, the highest form of creative expression known to Man.

Man's awareness of his Veritable Self, God-Consciousness and his oneness with the One Creative Consciousness, God, is intuitive. Man can accept the idea intellectually, but can *experience* God-Consciousness only spiritually. Then intellectual acceptance becomes conviction.

We are Companion-Vagabonds on the Joyous Journey to Joy-Age

Joy-Age, in the Idiom of Joy-Age, is the "Kingdom of Heaven" which is within. Although we are *within* the Kingdom of Heaven or Joy-Age constantly, we do not experience it consciously until we realize this, or "recognize the scenery," like Vagabonds who pass from one country to another but do not know it until they read the Road-Signs.

God-Consciousness, which is the "Kingdom of Heaven," is within us but we are within the "Kingdom of Heaven" as the deep-sea fishes are within the sea and the sea is within the deep-sea fishes.

We are *One-in-Spirit.* We are individual-in-experience as our *Human or Seeming-Selves,* as each finger is an individual area-of-sense-of-touch yet all are "hand," and "hand" is only an area of body given over to its separate activities, yet in no wise separate from "body."

In our Veritable Selves we are One-as-Many and Many-as-One.

This Spirit-Brotherhood goes beyond appearance;

This Spirit-Brotherhood goes beyond blood lines.

This Spirit-Brotherhood goes beyond personalities and form.

We are, indeed, Companion-Vagabonds.

Greetings, Companion-Vagabonds.

Aloha oe.

ONE

There is the Presence, vast and intimate,
  Substance of cell and star, power of heart,
  A Unity of All, no separate part;
The small is great with greatness of the Great
To be, to grow, to vision, to create.

Power of Presence in the tidal flow
  Of seas . . . and in the ebb and flow of blood;
  The same impulse that makes the violets bud
Gives giantcy to redwoods as they grow.
A Cosmic Plan that makes one *thus,* one *so.*

One urge, one mind, one fatherhood of birth,
  One energy throughout, from seed to fruit;
  Unfoldment from within, vast and minute,
The farthest nebula, the clod of earth,
Growth that is mingled agony and mirth.

One heartthrob in the man, the fish, the brute.
  One magnet drawing all to one far Goal,
  The cell, the atom and the human soul.
One Song, the thunder-song, the warbler's flute,
The rock-song, slow, encenturied and mute.

Ask of the sprouting seed why it must grow.
  Why must the singer sing, the dancer dance?
  Why must my wild swan heart search the expanse
Of pathless skies for paths where it must go?
God knows! The Power-Presence, God, *does know.*

JOY IS DYNAMIC

Finger the word "Joy" with your thoughts. Feel the tingle of its dynamic infectious energy. It is a *force* as real as electricity.

Toss the word "Joy" around in your mind to know its buoyant lift. Chew the word "Joy" like a nourishing morsel for the vitamins of well-being resultant from assimilating its stimulation. It *is* a force. Turn the word "Joy" like a lozenge on your tongue. Taste its spiced syllables. During the enjoyment of Joy we are transformed, literally.

The *emotion*, Joy, is usually inarticulate.

Speechless with Joy	*Bursting with Joy*	*Radiant with Joy*
Nearly died of Joy	*Shouted with Joy*	*Eyes shining with Joy*
Wept happily for Joy	*Incoherent with Joy*	*Danced for Joy*
Leaped with Joy	*Tingled with Joy*	*Rosy with Joy*

The therapy of Joy . . . anything which can produce the results above . . . is as powerful as any drug. Use it wisely. It is always available.

When we learn that our Checking Account of Joy is in the Inexhaustible Reserve of Creative God-Consciousness we will dare to *spend* our Joy, our Time, our Selves freely and generously rather than meagerly in thin timorous pennies and dimes. *We will not hoard.*

Remember the inarticulate gasp of Joy when, as a child, you saw the long-desired and long-anticipated toy on the Christmas tree?

Remember the first kiss which was a real depth-bomb?

Remember the impact of Joy the first time you hit the center of the bull's-eye in archery? Remember the first "strike" of a big fish, and the second tug of Joy when you landed it? Remember the uprush of Joy and honest pride the first time you heard the words, "Well done, Son?"

All of these are inarticulate and dynamic reactions.

But, you might say, *"You can't just turn on Joy like a light."*
You do not doubt, when you turn the switch, that the light will radiate from the light globe, because you know of the great dynamos.

Have equal or greater reliance on the inexhaustible power of the Presence of Creative God and you will never doubt your Joy-Supply.

Joy is beyond words. Ah-h-h-h-h! The gasp. The long-drawn sigh. The silent shining. The dawning of realization. The radiance of acceptance. The experience. Oh-h-h-h-h! Joy! The artesian flow.

Sometimes we discover the New Adventure
In the Unknown Lands of our Inner Life
And have a Great Romance
With our Veritable Selves.

TUMBLEWEED TRAIL

We travel light . . . we Tumbleweeds,
Many our *wants* but few our *needs*.
    What do we carry in our pack?
    Little to burden a Roamer's back,
A compass, not in the hand but heart,
The sweat-stained folds of a faded chart
    That tells of Treasure buried far
On a nameless isle where a cryptic scar
On a fallen tree gives the Secret Clue
To the hiding place. And what do we do
    With the loot when it's ours to have and hold?
    We trade it in for the mad Fool's Gold
Of another Dream and another Quest. . . .
There is no rootage, there is no rest.
    Treasure Found is the lesser part
For a Son of Dust with Tumbleweed Heart.

I'd rather be hungry, with not-quite-enough
Than sated . . . and have to keep gorging the stuff.

ROAD-SIGN. Life simplifies when we learn the difference between
"I want" and *"I need."* Willie *wants* to eat green apples. Willie will
need the bathroom.

JUNIOR IS BORN

I helped to birth a baby.
It was an emergency.
I was an Innocent Bystander.
I got drafted.
Out of the experience, five pictures developed in the Candid Camera
of my memory.
I shall never forget them.
I want never to forget them.
They were . . . The Emergence,
The Severing of the Cord,
The Cry,
The Clutching Hands,
And The Answer.

> There were four of us in the room.
> Suddenly there were five.
> An icy finger of awe went up my spine.
> Destiny had entered that small stuffy room.

This Squirming Mite might become a Great Leader, A Great Tyrant
or a Great Almost-Anything, or only one of the Human Cover-Crop
plowed under without fame to make soil for the MIP (More Important
People).

> It was my job to cut the cord.
> I remember saying . . .
> *"Junior, you're on your own now.*
> *You're alone.*
> *It's rather terrifying, isn't it?"*

Junior's answer was a thin wail which carried inarticulate fright.
*I did not then know that before long I would be echoing that frightened
cry.*

> The small red hands waved in space
> And clutched at Nothingness.

*I did not then know that soon I would be waving desperate hands in
space and clutching at Nothingness.*

> My Doctor Friend said, "Now you're going to see something so beau-
> tiful that, even after forty years of seeing it, I cry inside."

Junior was cleaned up, primped and taken to his Mother.
He was whimpering softly.
His Mother's arms moved to shape a protecting, enveloping curve.
Junior was placed in that Haven-Heaven-Curve.
Junior sighed.
His sigh was echoed by all of us.
It seemed that Universe Itself sighed.
The physical cord was severed.
It would never be rejoined.
But we saw Creator, Creation and Created fused into Oneness again.
There was such Peace in that room that it was luminous.
This Peace included us all.
The Return to the Source.
The Completed Circle
The Prodigal . . . Home.
Junior was not alone.
You are not alone.
I am not alone.
How long it takes to know that!
How terribly long.

QUENCHED THIRST

If you are thirsty you do not want an article *about* water, nor a
chemical analysis of water. You want the *experience of water.*
Quenched Thirst.   If you are ill you want healing.
I might give you a glass of water . . . *but I can not drink for you.*
It would be better if I pointed and said,
"There is The Spring. Drink for yourself."
All that anyone can say is, *"I drank from This Spring. My thirst
was quenched. Here it is."*
Thousands of books, and uncounted and uncountable billions of
words have gone into trying to explain God.
God can not be explained. God can not be packaged in words.
God-Consciousness must be experienced.   How?
This is an experience unique with each seeker.
The Spring will be found where the Thirst begins. Within.

I CHOOSE JOY

Are we like pliant clay shaped by our moods
To masks of gladness or to grief that broods
In fixed persistence on some long-past sorrows?
I say that we are sculptors of our morrows.
Our thoughts are fingers, masters of the clay,
And we can mold the masks we wear today.

Are we dumb goblets curved to hold a wine
Poured by the whims of Fate? *I say that mine*
Is the hand to choose the vintage, mine the hand
To judge the pouring, bitter, sweet or bland.
My thoughts the cellar where the wines are stored,
And I the one who chose the vinous hoard
Against the hour of need for friendly cheer.
I pressed the grapes; I brewed the lusty beer,
Unknowing often, yet with knowing choice,
I can select the mood-wine to rejoice
The passing hour, or drain the murky dregs . . .
Or brew new wine of Joy to fill the kegs.

Are we the painter or the canvas stretched
In acquiescence to the picture sketched
By careless hands of Chance? *I say that we*
Are canvas and *the painter.* We are free
To choose our thoughts like colors which we place
In careful sequence on the palette's space
To paint the murals of our passing day
In lapis, rose and gold . . . or weary gray.
God's patience waits through Time's vast timeless span
For Man to claim and use his Heritage. . . .
God-powered to shape the clay, to write the page.
When will we know Ourselves as . . . God-in-Man?

JOY IS A FACE-LIFT

Try this experiment with Joy.
No plastic surgeon could give you such a face-lift.
  Go to the mirror.
  Let your features hang down like wet wash on a rainy day.
  Wipe your face clean of expression.
  Become receptive, acquiescent, responsive, expectant.
Begin *thinking* of Joy . . . as an emanation of an actual healing *force*.
Think of some of its meanings.
"The anticipation or acquisition of good."
"The artesian uprush of happy gratefulness for fulfilled desire."
Try feeling good, *way out to here* . . . twenty feet in every direction.
Open your heart and let Spring blow through you like a fresh breeze.
Form the word "Joy" with your lips *but do not speak it yet.*
  Watch the animation spread over your features.
  Watch your eyes begin to light up like fireflies at dusk.
  Watch the smile-lines spread, lifting, *lifting* the features.
  Now say the word "Joy" softly. Then say it with increasing zest.
    Joy. Joy. J O Y.
The plainest faces become pleasant to look at when the word "Joy"
is animating them.
Young ladies of the Victorian Era were instructed to enter a room with
the words "prunes and prisms" on their lips, as it made their mouths
look more kissable. Many photographers suggest that the sitter say the
word "cheese" at the moment of shooting the picture. It is supposed to
shape the mouth to pleasant smiling lines.
  Try the word "Joy."
In prairie days of my youth we used to have to *"prime the pump"* with
water to get water from the well.
  The word "Joy" is a pump-primer to persuade Joy to come forth from
the deep well of potential happiness within us.
  The artesian well of Joy never runs dry. We clog it with our thoughts.
  The word "Joy" is the drill to penetrate to the artesian flow.
  Joy is not the fire-cracker, but the power which explodes it.
  Joy is *not* the blood-of-life, Joy *is* the power which pulses it.

TELESCOPE PEAK

Often and often in dreams, far away,
    I have visioned a mountain I seek.
Men who climb mountains will know what I say
    When I tell them of "Telescope Peak."
High and forbidding, a challenge, a fang,
    A snarl of defiance, a call
That sounds in the heart like a gong's strident clang
    To scale the white barrier-wall.

Good is the weariness, slumber and rest
    After the toil of the climb.
Good is the cleansing, the thrill of the crest
    After the sweat and the grime.
Rhythms of weariness . . . rhythms of quest,
    Toiling reiterant chime.
Victory . . . challenge . . . victory . . . rest . . .
    Challenge renewed . . . and the climb!

Climb it. Defy it. Achieve to the height.
    Savor the conqueror's zest.
Listen! A rushing . . . a dazzle of white,
    And above you . . . *a new gleaming crest*.
It rises in glory, a sword and a grail . . .
    A siren, a shrine and a wraith,
Urging the climber of mountains to scale
    With the scourge and the staff of this Faith.

Higher and higher and ever beyond . . .
   Each summit *a goal and a start.*
And ever and ever the climbers respond
   To the lure of the vanishing chart.
Often and often in dreams far away
   I vision this mountain I seek.
Men who climb mountains will know what I say
   When I tell them of . . . Telescope Peak.

When Mount Everest is climbed . . . *and it will be climbed . . .*
many Men Who Climb Mountains will feel a conflict of emotions. They
will feel a great rejoicing that one of their Breed has achieved the highest . . . and a sick regret that now, *now,* there is no longer a Higher
Peak, at least on this Earth of ours.

But they will find more and more-difficult ways to climb the peak
because they want the Climb. For the Searcher-Heart it is true that
Treasure Found is Less Than Treasure Sought.

My good friend, Lyle Brigham, of Bend, Oregon, has a passion for
climbing mountains, or rather a passion for climbing mountains *has him.*

Why? A dozen answers will crowd from his lips, and then a grin.
"There's just something about mountains," he will say.

"There's just something within him," is the answer.

There is something within us which, sooner or later, drives us to the
search for We-Know-Not-What. Is it the Search For God?

Who has seen God?

It is the hunger for *realization of God.*

Though we stay at Home or go to the deeps of the Pacific or the peak
of Mount Everest, or the depths of the Ocean . . . that which we seek
is always *with us, within us.*

We climb to the mountain peak of our own Inner Lives and find there
. . . *ourselves,* our *Veritable Selves.*

After the finding . . . do we rest?

The Peak Within is Telescope Peak, always extending beyond and
above, always challenging, always beckoning.

How splendid.

A Certain Rich Young Man of America set out to climb one of our great peaks in the West, without a guide. He fell and was killed. Thoughtless people said, "The poor fool, when he could get anything that money can buy, what did he want to kill himself on a mountain for?"

This, The Climb, *was something that money could not buy. No one could say that he bought his way to the top. Like all of the* "gallant frantic fools" *of all times he gambled his life for a priceless intangible. Who can say that he lost?*

RIDDLE

Why did you climb the mountain, Son? What did you go to seek?
>> *Fame, perhaps in the eyes of men,*
>> *Pictures to paint, poems to pen,*
>> *Flaming words to speak?*
>>> I brought not even a pebble down,
>>> A crumbled jewel from the Monarch's crown,
>>> And yet, I found the thing I sought,
>>> For what I sought and found I brought
>>>> Up and down the peak.
>>> Yet, what I found I could not see,
>>> Time and Space and Infinity,
>>> Three in One and One in Three,
>>> I in Them and They in Me.
>> This I learned on the mountain peak.
>> *I am* the thing I seek.

THE SELECTIVE HEART

You might reasonably say, "But we can't just BE joyful to order."
  Why not?
Why is it so easy to BE blue . . . to BE bored . . . to BE anxious
without any immediate traceable cause? These moods sneak up on us.
  You might say, "Oh, well, with the world-picture as it is,
  Of course, it is easy to be anxious and blue."
  Certainly it is.
But, with the world-picture as it is,
Is there any lack of beauty, of abundance in the earth?
There are more roses than skunks in the world. But . . .
Because the *skunk smells louder,* we notice the skunk
And sometimes forget the roses.
  A Chinese friend of mine said that he had a "selective nose."
  In the market there was a shelf.
  On top of the shelf there were rows of narcissi in bowls.
  Below the shelf were tubs of fish in brine.
  I could not enjoy the blossoms for the fish.
When my Chinese friend shopped for fish, he was *fish-conscious.*
When he shopped for narcissi he was *perfume-conscious.*
He had a "selective nose."
  We are easily bored, anxious, blue, because these are surface emotions.
  They come from John Ego Adamsmith's illusion of separateness-
  through-humanness.
  Actually we are "Joy-full or Joy-filled,"
  Just as we are "Life-full or Life-filled,"
  By the sheer act of living.
  The debris and silt of human thinking clogs the outlet
  for the artesian flow of Joy from the deep Source within.
We have "selective hearts" if we but know it.
  With my "selective heart," I choose JOY.

HALO

A halo circled the great white star
    That burned over Bethlehem.
Only the Wise Men from afar
    Knew what it said to them;
It said, "In the hearts of men afar
    On many a distant morn
My light will shine on a tinsel star,
    On a bauble to adorn
The Feasts of Joy . . . and only the Wise,
    The Weary Ones and Forlorn
Will see that the halo that light their eyes
    Is a luminous Crown of Thorn.

COLORED SLIDES

A white beam of light from a projection machine penetrates the darkness of the room. It strikes the silver surface of a Screen. Colored slides are put into the beam of light. They appear on the screen. A child or a savage might think the pictures are the things pictured. If the scene appears upside down the child might try to right it by turning the screen over. It is told that an old Prospector, seeing his first movie, shot the villain on the screen for abusing Li'l Nell.

Consciousness is the beam of white undifferentiated light. The opinions, prejudices, fears, passions and dreams of John Ego Adamsmith make the colored slides which are thrown on the Screen of his human consciousness. Romeo Lancelot Hamm, with his emotionalism, vanity and touchiness, colors and discolors those slides.

Too often we, as John Ego Adamsmith, try to "right" the upside-down picture on the screen by turning the screen over, instead of going to the source, removing the slide and putting it in right-side-up.

We fight appearance. We shoot the villain "on the screen." We fight ghosts.

Aunt Cally used to say, "Ghosts is *nothin'* actin' like *somethin'*."

BIG

A young mother and her toddler son approached the General Sherman Tree in Sequoia National Park. The General Sherman tree is the oldest and greatest living thing in the world, so far as we know.

It is thirty-two and a half feet through. It is over 3500 years old. Its top branches ensnare clouds. A man is diminished to insect size in its presence.

These dimensions mean little until we have "experienced the tree."

The small boy's eyes started at the base of the tree and climbed and climbed.

His face became rapt with delight.

Here was something satisfyingly huge.

Here was bigness beyond Daddy's bigness.

Here was bigness beyond an elephant's bigness.

He breathed the greatest poem that was ever written about the General Sherman Tree.

"B I G," he said in hushed wonderment.

The whispered word expanded to include the great tree and spread beyond and above it.

His lips formed the word again: "B I G."

For a moment the great tree and the very small boy spoke to each other in silent communion. A communion deeper than the word.

> Mother, in well-intentioned determination to improve the shining moment, said, "It's a TREE, Junior. Say 'TREE.'"
>
> Junior said "TREE."
>
> "It's a Sequoia Tree," said Mother. "Say SEE-QUOY-YAH."
>
> Junior said "SEE-QUOY-YAH."
>
> "That's what we build houses of, Junior. Say 'HOUSES.'"
>
> Junior said "HOUSES" with diminishing interest.
>
> "And that's what we make matches of, and match boxes," said Mother. "Say 'MATCHES and MATCH BOXES.'"

Junior looked at Mother with deep, bewildered resentment.

Something wrong was happening.

Someone was stealing his "B I G" from him.

Mother was cutting his tree down and making matches and match boxes with it.

Junior saw a chipmunk.

Before Mother could further destroy his "BIG" he scampered away.
He paused.

Mother was reading some statistics about the tree from a poster.

Junior's lips silently formed the word "B I G."

But it wasn't quite as big as before.

WHERE THE SUN SETS

I used to watch the Indians of Taos on their terraced earth-homes
at sunset time. Several of them stood, statue-silhouettes against the
turquoise sky through the sunset and afterglow.

The wine of sunset stained the folds of their blankets with crimson.
Something was happening to those immobile figures. *I envied them.*
After months of cautious approach I questioned one of the young men.
I can't give you his slow words but I can pass-along his Patrin.

"You white people like to put things into words and into books.
You watch the sunset and say, 'It is beautiful. It is red and yellow
and orange. The earth is turning and so the sun seems to go down.'
You are so busy putting the sunset into words that you *don't experience
the sunset.   Let the sun set inside of you! Let it stay there.* Later
you will want to *give that sunset to a friend.* The words will come.
You will paint the sunset which is *inside of you* more beautifully than
that sunset that you paint while you watch it. I have seen that happen
with you artists."

He continued, "I let the sun set *inside me.* I am silent about it.
Sometime later when we Indians get together for a "sing" in the
evening, the sunset will come forth as a song. Perhaps that song
will go into our tribe's remembered music. Children many generations
away will *see that sunset.*"

Be still and know. Be still and experience the knowing. Hold that *knowing* until it has inundated your whole being. Speak of it only to pass-it-
along. Then, in giving it you will keep it.

Loneliness and Aloneness are occupational hazards
of living in our Contemporary age.
To the Lonely and Alonely Ones I say . . .
"We need not be lonely. We are not alone . . ."

THIS BOOK IS FOR YOU IF YOU ARE . . .

A VAGABOND . . . lured ever on and on by the vision of a Splendor-
       Land somewhere,

A TUMBLEWEED . . . Faithful to faithlessness of all save far hori-
        zons.

A MAVERICK . . . Immune to any brand, scornful of fences.

A SEARCHER . . . Who knows that Treasure Found is less than
       Treasure Sought.

THE HUNGRY-HEARTED . . . Rebel to adhesive loves; never too
         much possessing, never too much possessed.

THE UNCOMPASSED . . . Whose hearts are fixed on no fixed star.

THE DRIFTWOOD . . . Who know that only change is constant.

THE FLOTSAM and THE JETSAM . . . The Scattered Brother-
        hood who have one pass-word, "QUEST."

     Aloha . . . from a Blood Brother.

This book is for the Ones who gambled all
 On *Love* . . . and lost; or winning, could not hold;
 Who took the glinting tinsel for the gold;
Or waited, lonely, for the mating call
Which did not come; who feared *Love's* sacrifice
 Or were too humble to stretch out a hand
 Or bound *Love* with a too-adhesive band,
Or, being hurt, dared not to venture twice

On that uncertain road without a chart.
    This book would say, "The Search is not in vain.
    There is an Inner Joy to ease the pain
And quench the fevers of the Thirsting Heart."

Perhaps you descend from the Line of the Prodigal Son. Most of us do.

This book is for the Ones who gambled all
    On *Pleasure,* using senses for the coin;
    Who pawned their years for money to rejoin
The Revelers who watch the quick dice fall
In patterned Chance, oblivious of the hour
    When Shylock will demand his pound of flesh;
    This book would tell the Ones caught in the mesh
Of *Pleasure's* usury. "There is a Power,
Kinder than Justice, greater than harsh Fate.
    Oh, Prodigals, who seek the homeward road,
    Wearied with dark Regret's increasing load,
That Power will slow the closing of the Gate.

You will probably find yourself in this group, the largest of all.

This book is for the Ones who gambled all
    On *Happiness* and built a House of Dreams,
    Trusting too much the strength of fragile beams
Fashioned from aspen, willow-weak, to fall
When storms of sterner days and winds of night
    Joined with the armies of the testing gales
    To shake the walls and pull the shallow nails
Of wishes unsupported by the might
Of Faith. This book would say, "Oh, do not fear.
    There is an Architect in whom to trust
    To build beyond the power of storm and rust.
Friend, dare to build again when He says, "Here."

MONKEY BUSINESS

There are times when I can well believe
That we descend from monkeys. I perceive
My restless simian fingers pluck the thread
That ravels my Life's strong fabric stained with red
Of Heart's-blood and with Faith's strong blue.
Why must my Left Hand endlessly undo
My Right Hand's weaving. Is there a tailless ape,
A Dark Twin caged inside my brain to jape
And jibber in its boredom as I go
Back to the Loom to weave again with slow
And wearied patience? Surely there is a Cause
(*I must believe*) why thoughtless monkeys' paws
Are gloved within our God-creative hands.
There is, I hope, a Presence that understands.

We can destroy our Happiness, our Pleasure,
But Joy, Thank God, is like a buried treasure
So wisely and so skillfully concealed
That only hints are frugally revealed
Of its abundance. Then, when we give up
The Search, a random coin or golden cup
Lures us to Seeking. Maybe it is well
That Those-Who-Know *can not* or *will not* tell
Why like a weary metronome we sway
Forward and back and forward, day by day,
The Man and Ape in conflict in our hands.
I know a Presence sees and understands.

**** **** **** *°**

The Fall of Man occurs daily, hourly or as often as John Ego Adamsmith takes the First Personal Singular Pronoun "I" and applies it to
his Personal Human or Seeming Self instead of realizing that his Only
Veritable Self is the "I" of God's "I AM." In God-Consciousness we live,
move and have our being. There is not All *and* something else.

Why does John Ego Adamsmith with his Adam-hand destroy the
work of his Veritable Self? Why the Monkey Business? We don't have
to be that way.

[76]

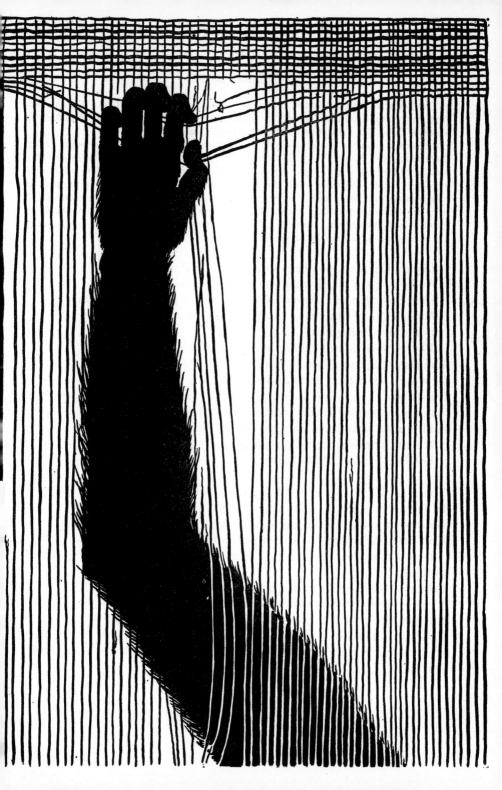

PEELED ZERO

*The Jewel of Faith is found in strange places. We look for it in a Tiffany set-
ting, forgetting that the diamond is found in the ground, or as a rough pebble in
a gravel heap. Its brilliance depends on cutting and polishing.*

*I found a jewel of the first water in a smoker of a little train between Tulsa,
Oklahoma, and Kansas City, Missouri. Two porters were talking religion. One
was an older man with a quiet sure faith which did not question. The other was
a younger man, educated with that dangerous "little knowledge" so typical of
this generation's teachings. The younger man was sniping at the older man's faith
with all of the specious arguments current these days. Finally the older man went
quiet. I had lived among these people and I knew that the quiet man was getting
his A-bomb ready. Finally he spoke . . . and WITH AUTHORITY.*

Lissen, Cepheus, you been away to college
And you got a lot of what you *calls* knowledge.
But, Boy, that ain't *knowledge* . . . that's just *book-learning,*
Knowledge is what your heart *knows* concerning
Folks and loving and living.
There's less talk of *taking* and more of *giving*.
You may think you's what you calls a *ay-the-ist*
Or a Egg-nos-tick. I don't know what a *nog* is,
But I knows a *egg* when I sees one, and I knows a *bad egg* when I smells it,
There's *something* in this room that *ain't* perfume.
And it ain't emanating from me or that white gentleman.
It's the smell of them foul things you's a-saying.
Louder than a jackass braying.

You says that the Good Book is full of contradictions.
In fact, that it *begins* with a contradiction
Because it says, "In the beginning was the Word,"
And that a Word can't come out of *nothing*.
Boy, I just been listening to a mighty lot of words coming out of
nothing.
Because "Nothing" is *you* in your present frame of mind.
You's *nothing* trying to be *something*.
But you don't want to do *nothing* about being *something*.
You just goes around trying to make other folks *nothinger* than you is.
And the more *nothinger* that you is, the more *somethinger* you *thinks*
you is.

[78]

You know what you reminds me of?
In arithmetic they's got a little figure they calls a **Zeero**.
A Zeero is *Nothing* with a line around it.
Nothing with a line around it. That's your present frame of mind.
And you know what's happened to you?
You was up on the corner zeeroing at the top of your voice.
You was zeeroing at all the pretty girls passing by, and I don't blame
you for *that*.
But that Ol' Devil comes up behind you and sees this *bunch of nothing*
with a line around it called a Zeero.
And just like slipping the skin off of a grape, he skins that line from
around that Zeero.
And what's left?
        . . . A PEELED ZERO. Yessir, a PEELED ZERO.
Just a *big bunch of bare nothing* without even its underwear on.

And there ain't *nothing* in the world so cold and dismal and lone-
some as a *peeled Zeero*. *Nothing* around it. *Nothing* in front of it.
Nothing behind it. And giving off *nothing* in every direction.

I tells you what you gotta do, Boy, cause you's in a sad way. You
gotta get you some Faith.

How's you going to get what you ain't got and don't believe in any-
how? I'll tell you, Boy. *You's done it before.*

Remember when you was a little shaver? You went out to the Ole
Swimming Hole with the yuther boys. You sits on the bank, skeered stiff
of that old cold deep-looking water, because *you knows that you cain't
swim.*

But the yuther boys is in there snorting and cavorting, and you
wants to be *in the swim,* too. That's just human.

You puts your toe in. Then you gets knee-deep, then chin-deep and
finally you DUNKS.

It ain't so bad. But still *you knows that you don't know how to swim.*

You goes in for several days, and nobody don't know the time between
when you cain't and *when you can* swim. But the next day you goes in,
you takes a deep breath and *you submits yourself to the Element.*

And you SWIMS.

Boy, what a sensation! You's the swimmingest boy in that whole pud-
dle. Then you tries to get the yuther little fellers to try, cause that's getting Faith in a big way . . . you wants to share it . . . everywhere.

→

Then you know what happens? That old *peeled zeero* begins developing a skin around it again.

And you begins growing . . . up.

The old fat sides of that *zeero* begins slimming down . . . as the *hot air leaks out of it* . . . until there ain't no space between them two sides, and they lengthens right out into a straight up-and-down line. And you know what that straight line is?

It's the word "I."

Remember how Jesus said, "Before Abraham was, *I AM?*"

Well, now you's got the first part of "I AM."

When you gets the "AM" part you'll be a man grown. You'll be worth talking with then. Come back and see me.

In the meantime, God bless you, Boy. And Now get them shoes shined . . . and good.

TO KNOW A COUNTRY

Learn the slang of the country.
Eat the foods of the country.
Sing the songs of the country.
Play with the children of the country.
Shop with the housewives of the country.
Laugh with the young men of the country.
Work with the fathers of the country.
Listen to the old men of the country.
Live in a home of the country.
Love a woman of the country.

Speaking of "giving and taking," loneliness is often the result of bad bargaining. "I'll love you if you'll love me, but you love me first and most."

IMMENSITY

Remark often heard at the Ocean, Grand Canyon, Niagara Falls, Palomar Observatory and other publicized immensities: "It makes me feel so small and insignificant."

Why should you and I feel small
Before Niagara's mighty fall?
   The great cascade which never stops
   Is *only* endless trillion drops
   Moving in one splendid mass.
   Time is seconds as they pass.
   Grand Canyon . . . only emptiness
   Where what was *much* is now *much less,*
   As scrillion-billion grains of sand
   Got bored with merely *being land*
   And plunged into the river's race
   To . . . *go be land some other place.*   *(How human!)*

   Humanity is only *us*
   In *Time's* majestic calculus.
   Many you-and-I together
   Bound by patriotic tether
   Make our nation great or small.
   United . . . stand. Divided . . . fall.
   We know that one and one make two;
   Since two is made by me-and-you,
   And two and two add up to four,
   And five times four makes up a score,
   And scores of scores increase so quick
   Well . . . you know your arithmetic.
   Let's not forget . . . *immensity*
   Is *simply lots of you-and-me.*

Measured by the pound we, you and I and John Ego Adamsmith and Jane Ego Evesmith, are very small dust. We should indeed feel futile and insignificant. But that is not the way we are measured. In our Immortal Veritable Selves we are all that we see, all that we know, all that we experience. With our Selective Hearts we may choose that with which we identify ourselves. That is our good fortune, but too often we are Heirs to a Fortune and unaware of it.

I AM NOT A PERSON

At the time when I realized that, regardless of its value as a book, this book must be done if I hoped to achieve any peace of mind, I was badly puzzled. In all humility I realized that in my Personal Self I was not capable of saying the things which I hoped to say, a problem not new to those who try to pass-along the Spiritual Vision which has come to them and which they wish to share.

One night, before I achieved sleep belatedly, I had been talking with that Shadowy Mysterious Self which all of us admit that we have when we say, "I said to myself . . ."
"Who says what to whom . . . and who listens?"
Who is the "I?" Who is the "Myself?"
I call this hovering Other Self *"Silent Partner."*
Said I, *"Silent Partner,* where does this bundle of talents, hopes, doubts, emotions, intuitions, hunches, yearnings and anxieties which seem to be 'I' fit into the scheme of things so that I don't feel as futile as confetti in a typhoon? *Give me a lead. Give me guidance."*

The answer, felt and sensed but not spoken, came, *"Don't worry. There is an answer. You'll find it."*

In the morning I half-wakened. My body was still in deep repose. In my Conscious Self I seemed to be waiting to put on the Garment of Body for the day, but was enjoying that quiet interval of freedom when things seem to be seen with a new clarity.

I heard my own voice speaking, clearly in a level tone, but without my Conscious Volition. It was saying in French, *"Je ne suis pas une personne. Je suis seulement une articulation pour la beauté dans mes abilities d'écrire, de parler, de peintre et . . . de vivre."*

"I am not a person. I am solely an articulateness for beauty through my abilities to write, to speak, to paint and . . . (long pause) to live."

There it was!

I was to accept the fact that, during this period at least, I was not to be a person but an articulateness within the limits of my abilities for this experience which, regardless of how insignificant it might appear to others, was a tremendous one in my own life.

I remembered a line from the teachings of Joel Goldsmith in his

Infinite Way classes. "Get rid as soon as you can of a sense of Personal Existence."

The two thoughts fused. And I remembered a third teaching which I had found, I don't recall where. *"We do not choose our talents. They choose us."*

Similar words had been said two thousand years ago, to a group of men who were chosen to be "articulateness" for a message which was to change the life of our world.

The old Ego, ever on the defensive against any loss of its territory, offered persuasive argument, "You'll simply be a zombie, an ectoplasm. You'll be amorphous . . . and that is just a squashed morph."

But there were the orders. I accepted them, but I did not know how to obey. At my desk a few hours later I found the New Testament among my reference books immediately at hand. I opened the pages at random, so it seemed. From the pages leaped these lines to signal my eyes,

"And he taught them many things by parables."

Parables, poems, paradoxes, patrin, pointers, puzzles, pass-alongs, of course! That which can not be explained may be implied, pointed out, put in parables and puzzles so that the Searcher, when he has found the concealed thought, may claim it as "his."

This book is my honest attempt to pass-along to you the Road-Maps which set me on the Joyous Journey to Joy-Age (whatever your age, your Joy-Age is now . . . if you can realize it).

Whether I have failed or succeeded . . . I have tried.

I could not give you my joy if I would.
I would not give you my joy if I could.
   Your joy must be woven *by* you, *for* you.
   The warp and the woof will be your heartstrings
   And the days of your days.
It must be tailored *for* you, *by* you,
If it is to fit you like the warm strong garment that it is.
   I can not give you what you have already.

JOYFUL RENDEZVOUS

So many I have loved are gone . . . are gone,
   Carl, Scotty, Earl, Cerise, Maje, Father, Mother,
   Prent, Andy, Bart and Jim, the Prodigal Brother,
Somewhere between the Sunset and the Dawn.
Yet, are they gone? All that I have loved in them
   I have . . . a splendid nearness, strangely real . . .
   The heart-leap quickened to recalled appeal
Of laughter, tenderness. No requiem
Sounds in the heart for dear departed ghosts
   Withdrawn from touch of hands and tender lips,
   Yet, not beyond the hearts' companionships . . .
More real than all the harried, hurried hosts
That crowd the blur of jet-propulsioned days,
   Meeting and greeting, chatting and scatting on,
   Tossing confetti-words hither-and-yon,
Warming our fingertips from sparks that blaze
Like paper fires, bright yet all too brief.
   Which are the ghosts . . . the quick or those called "dead?"
   With eyes washed clear of mists by tears long-shed
Let me look through the curtainings of grief.

They are all here! How could I make them wait
   Outside a door seal-locked by false despair?
   Turn on the light, make soft the easy-chair,
Toss driftwood powder on the embered grate.
Come in, dear Vagabonds. The wasted years
   Are gone, forgotten. Here is our endless *now*.
   A toast to you . . . and me . . . and us. *Here's how!*
Forgive and understand these joyful tears.

*John Ego Adamsmith and Jane Ego Evesmith are vividly aware of Past, and
equally vividly uneasy about Future. But so often they live the splendid* Now
without conscious awareness that it has neither beginning nor end.

   *The Veritable Self knows nothing of "Then." The Veritable Self knows nothing
of "There." Only HERE and NOW.*

   *"They are all here!" Of course, where "they" have always been, in my heart and
mind.*

THE GAME OF HOT OR COLD

When I was young we played a childish game,
Called "Hot or Cold," I think that was its name.
At any rate, as I recall the plot,
We hid an object in some secret spot
Then gave the Seeker clues by calling out,
"Warm . . . warmer," as he neared, or warning shout,
Of "Cold . . . colder" as he strayed away.
  I got a funny-wise idea one day
  That Life will play the game of "Hot or Cold"
  With us if we will listen when we're told,
  "Warm . . . warmer . . . cold or colder." All the clues
  Are there to find if we will only use
  Our eyes for seeing and our ears to hear.
The Silent Voice says "Warmer" as we near
The Hidden Goal, or "Colder" as we seek
Afar on some vast distant mountain peak
For that which hides within our Secret Heart.
  Life gives the clues if we will do our part
  And look . . . and listen, heeding words, "Be still
  And know."   We follow will-o'-the-wisps until
  We weary in confusion and despair,
  Then hear the Silent Voice say, "Here . . . not There
Is what you seek, for *I AM* where *you are*.
I AM the Life that guides the shining star.
I AM the Life within the patient seed,
I AM the Answer to your crying need,
I AM the Nameless One with many names,
I AM the Spark that lights the heart to flames.
I AM the Atom and the farthest blue,
I AM the You behind the transient you,
I AM the Clod . . . and seed within the Clod . . .
I AM . . . God."

THREE EARS

I have three ears. By that I mean
The Right and Left with *me* between
Which seems the standard style in ears . . .
The usual outside pair that hears
The thunder and the rusty cricket
Or linnet's carol in the thicket,
The tyrant clock, policeman's whistle,
The pair of curving flesh and gristle.
They're nothing special, large and clean,
The Right and Left . . . with *me* between.

The Other Ear . . . I'm not sure where . . .
Hears Silence waiting on a stair
For footsteps which must surely sound;
It hears the growingness of ground,
It hears the twilight seeping in
And blood's not pulsing under skin.
It hears the dawn break on the sky
And Time's soft rustle slipping by.
It hears a poem being born
And fraying heart-strings as they're torn.
It hears the star-dust drifting down
Like silver snowflakes on the town.
   It hears that Voice, so deep and low,
   Which councils me, *"Be still and know."*

Prayer is not what we say to the Presence, but what the Presence tells us in a voice of muted thunder or in a whisper with the cutting edge of a ghost-razor. Wordless and thought-less, the "Knowing" comes to us when we are stilled and receptive.

SONS OF DUST

With our focus-of-awareness in our *Human or Seeming-Selves* we are Sons of Dust, John Ego Adamsmith or Jane Ego Evesmith.

As Sons of Dust we are subjects of the Kingdom of Flesh-Awareness, and, as such, subject to the laws of perishable flesh, *so long as we remain in this focus-of-awareness.*

> You and I, in our Human or *Seeming-Selves* are like a child born and reared on the floor of a deep circular valley, with no one to inform us of the World-Beyond-The-Valley. We would not know of the great plains stretching away to the horizons. Our horizon would be above our eye level and limited to the circle of the valley's rim.

Perhaps we hear rumors of this "Land Beyond." We scale the walls of the valley. We come onto the plains. We feel that *now* we have found Released Horizons. The Plains-People know *only the plains.* They do not know of the great mountains far beyond the edge of the sky.

As we find freedom from the Closed Horizons of the valley we know a strange irresistible restlessness. We journey toward the West. We look up at great peaks. We do not yet know of the Expanded Horizons which await the Scalers of Peaks.

We climb the peaks. We see in the blue distance a greater blueness which beckons to us. We follow the far call. We come to the sea. Horizons push back farther and farther. We board ship to follow the Retreating Horizons.

> In the small ship we follow the sun until land is almost a forgotten thing. There are no companion ships. We are surrounded by Nothing-but-Nothingness.
>
> *Surely here we will find Released Horizons.*

Yes, horizons retreat before us, but as we look back we find the horizons following us, *relentlessly, eternally closing in.*

The Divine Claustrophobia makes us seek a sky-climbing plane which takes us higher than man has ever flown before. But always we are inclosed in a vast blue capsule, immaterial but real. We are still Prisoners-of-the-Senses.

In the Realm-of-the-Intellect we seek freedom. We find, however, that we can only think *about* Released Horizons. We have not experienced them.

In despair we close our eyes, shutting out the Visible Horizons. We acknowledge defeat.

With our fears and our anxieties we draw the Inclosing Horizons about us until we are crushed by their enveloping immensity.

The Divine Claustrophobia gives us strength to be Samsons and we push back with a strength beyond our knowing.

In that moment we move into God-Consciousness.

Wordlessly and thought-lessly we *know*.

In God-Consciousness we ARE Universe.

In God-Consciousness we ARE Joy.

In God-Consciousness we ARE Life.

> We return to the land. We retrace our footsteps,
> up the peaks and down, across the plains to our
> deep valley.
> We are no longer Prisoners-of-Horizons.
> We have brought our Released-Horizons with us.
> We are one with the One Consciousness which is

emergent into individual consciousness, experiencing Itself in form and activity. We experience the realization of the Word, the Idea made Flesh. But we know now that in our oneness with the One Consciousness, God, we are eternally the Word, the Idea, the Life.

In the Truth *we have always been free*. In our *realization of the Truth* we now *know that we are free*.

> The Phantom Music sounds ever and always in the Tumbleweed Heart.
> It is unheard for long periods or heard so faintly that it is lost in the confusion of the clamorous senses and the insistencies of the arrogant intellect.
> But one day, one hour, one moment, in the stillness of desert,
> In the loneliness of sea or quiet moment in a room at dusk,
> It will sound, clear and unmistakable, the Phantom Music of Immortality
> Now.

SEED OF THE TUMBLEWEED

Within each of us, the most phlegmatic or the most volatile, we have the latent Seed of the Tumbleweed.

This Seed of the Tumbleweed may sprout at any time. As it grows, due to its shape, it is tugged at by the winds of restlessness. This is a restless desire for we-know-not-what at first.

It is a Divine Restlessness, a Spiritual Claustrophobia, which is a dread of being in closed rooms or narrow spaces, except, of course, the Narrow way which is "strait" in its limitations on side-wise ventures but endless in its "forward going" progression.

This Spiritual Claustrophobia will start us on our Journey to Joy-Age. It is the story of the Prodigal Son. We may wander in a long and wide circle before we find the End of the Search . . . Home. We have carried the Beginning and the End of the Search with us all the way, because that-which-we-sought was our Veritable Selves.

This restlessness may first find its release in physical adventure, travel, exploration, movement, under the delusion that places, people and things will "give" us security, happiness, peace. It is at this time that we Prodigals "go to Babylon." Babylon is neither good nor bad,

"When the tales of cities are told and ended . . .
People made them what they were . . . foul or splendid."

Later this restless seeking may lead us along the intellectual road, with curiosity and probings into philosophies, intellectual systems, rationalizations which seem to satisfy us for a while, but like certain foods, they have bulk and flavor but lack vitamins and minerals.

We can be as gluttonous with this dry fare as with sensual and sensuous indulgence. In time the taste of husks will come to our awareness. We find that we are feeding an insatiable tapeworm, with an appetite which grows with what it feeds on.

We find that we are vacuum cleaners, endlessly sucking in the dust of tangibles and inadequate philosophies until our intake is clogged.

The next move of the Tumbleweed Heart is an experience which comes to each of us in our own way and in our own time.

The divine Claustrophobia drives us into the wide Freedom of God-Consciousness, and freedom within the Law, Like the tight-rope walker, who has such amazing freedom of movement on the narrow rope through his *knowledge* and *use* of the inflexible law of gravity, we have freedom of movement by our knowledge and use of the Law of God-Consciousness in its uncountable diversifications of expression, yet oneness of principle.

PATRIN

WHAT IS THIS "JOY-AGE?"

You might ask, "What is this 'Joy-Age'?" Is it mysticism, New Thought, Mental Science, metaphysics, theosophy, another cult adding its confused voice to the ten thousand voices which proclaim *"This is the Way?"*

Say the word "blue" to a hundred people, and if you were able to see into the minds of the hundred people you would see a hundred shades of blue pictured there. I would have a picture of an oblong piece of lapis-lazuli which was given to me to remind me of the sea off Waikiki at a certain hour of a certain day. You might see the blue of desert skies if you were from Arizona. Another might see the beauty or the menace of a pair of blue eyes. One might see muted blue of dusk-sky which colored an exquisite hour.

Say the name "God" to a hundred people and there will be a hundred ideas of what *God is* and what *God is not.*

Regardless of declarations of faith, "God" is to each one *"God-as-each-one-understands-God."*

In a Search which was not casual, but was, in fact, desperate, I sought God, in the writings and teachings of many faiths.

Repeatedly I found a "Patrin" which seemed to guide me toward that "dynamic serenity," for me, my idea of "The Kingdom of Heaven."

PATRIN

"Patrin" (sometimes spelled *Patteran*) is a word I have always loved. Patrin; among Gypsies, a handful of leaves, grass or twigs, placed in certain understood designs beside the roads, especially at forks-of-the-roads, to say to those who follow on, "We went this way."

For me, the truest Patrin were placed along the Way by Jesus, with Christ-Consciousness. But even these wonderful Patrin were interpreted and misinterpreted so variously that confusion often followed.

One by one, I have found Patrin in the writings and teachings of many Companion-Vagabonds of the Road. I claim only this for them. *"They seemed to guide me to a peace of heart and mind which I have never known before but for which I desperately hungered."*

These Patrin, these handfuls of word-leaves, word-twigs, are merely passed-along to you, Companion-Vagabonds, in hope that they may serve you on your Way.

See pages 55 and 124 for lists of Patrin.

RAIN

For Carmen and Prentice who understand.

Water rose from Blue Ocean as Vapor.
For a while Water-as-Vapor drifted through Air.
Water-as-Vapor formed into Fluffy Cloud.
Wind and Sunlight played with Cloud.
Cloud expanded into soft beautiful forms tinted by Sunlight.
Rainbow curved a multicolored necklace for Cloud.
Cloud became vain and show-offy and forgot that it had ever been Ocean.
Wind's affection for Cloud chilled.
Wind blew coldly on Cloud to show its displeasure.
Cloud wept as Rain until it was no more Cloud.
Sunlight, being kinder than Wind, shone on Rain.
Rain glittered and sparkled like a jewel.
"How beautiful I am," said Rain, "I'm a jewel."
Rain forgot that it had been Cloud.
Rain saw a vast cold blueness below it.
"What is that," cried Rain, "that awful big cold blueness?"
Wind laughed, "That is Blue Ocean. You're going to fall into it and be lost . . . lost . . . lost in it."
"Oh, no," protested Rain. "I'm Jewel. I'm Rain. I'm beautiful. I don't want to be lost in Blue Ocean."
"Whether you like it or not," jeered Wind, "that's what's going to happen to you."
"Help me, help me!" cried Rain.
But Wind was off chasing Flying Fish across Blue Ocean.
Rain fell swiftly toward Blue Ocean.
Rain remembered that it had been Cloud and tried to turn back into Cloud. But it fell swifter and swifter.
Rain fell with a soft splash into Blue Ocean.
"Oh," cried Rain desperately. "Oh—oh . . .
And then, "Ah . . . I'm OCEAN."

Ancient Saying: *Rain Drop is not lost in Ocean; Ocean is found in Rain Drop. Soul is not lost in Eternity; Eternity is found in Soul.*

THE THINK GADGET

I think and I think and I *think* that I think
While the little wheels whir and the little lights blink;
There's a rattle, a humming, a rustle, a roar
And what do I get? What I got just before;
Some *more* thoughts to think about doodles and dancers,
So I think *some more thoughts* that I *think* are the answers.
But the *answers* breed *questions* . . . they're fertile as rabbits,
And I *think some more thoughts* about worries and habits,
As I moil and I toil and I fiddle and tinker . . .
And all that I get is a pain in my thinker.

Now, let me be still . . . oh, as still as a rock,
While I hear my heart beat like the tick of a clock,
And I feel the blood flow like the pulse of a tide,
Then I find that the answers are waiting . . . *inside.*
Not words . . . noisy words . . . but the luminous glowing.
The Light in the Shrine of the stillness of *knowing.*

The Ancients knew intuitively what the greatest scientists of today
are finding out experimentally in the laboratories and clinics, that the
"rabble of the senses and the arrogant intellect" can observe, conjecture
and deduce, but not truly *know,* any more than we can look into our own
eyes *with* our own eyes. We live our whole lives without ever seeing
what anyone else can see . . . our own faces. Reflections, yes, and
photographs, and such things . . . but not our own faces. It is under-
standable that the admonition "Know thyself" is so difficult to follow.
    The Veritable Self is experienced first and *known about* afterwards.
Seek the experience. How? *Find your roadmaps. Follow* them.

WHERE IS WONDER?

Where is wonder? Where is wonder *not?*
  From sun to atom, seed to mighty tree,
  The wonder of two tiny words, "to be"
And "to become"; the wonder of the plot
Which runs through Life, a thread unseen but sensed.
  I find it in this crab's claw on the sand
  Designed for purposed use as my own hand
Which holds the claw is purposed, flexed and tensed.

Where is wonder? Where is wonder *not?*
  This vast design in which no thing alone
  Is of itself a thing apart; unknown
Yet known to be, this Oneness of the clot
Of pulsant sperm with clots of starry dust
  Birthing new suns in dim celestial space,
  Revealing features of the faceless Face,
Evading mind yet stirring hearts to trust.

Where is wonder? Where is wonder *not?*
  Regard the lily! Watch as it responds
  To inner orders, as the curling fronds
Of ferns, all unresisting, ask not "what"
Nor "why." They *live* the prayer, "Thy will be done."
  Let it be so with me . . . let me *become*
  As clay yields to the sculptor's shaping thumb.
Rebellious Self, be still and know . . . the One.

[94]

LOST WONDER

I lost it for a while . . . the sense of Wonder,
  Caught in the rat-race, blinded by the smog
  Of small insistencies, the dusts that clog
The vital breath of Life. How did I blunder?
Futility, like the weary rains of winter,
  Subtle and penetrant, found the marrowed bone.
  The Guide Star blurred. Uncompassed and alone
I pinned Pride's shabby robe with frost's chill splinter.

The Winds of Time blew harshly, strangely colder.
  My forward gaze deflected to the ground.
  My feet refused the ceaseless, senseless round.
I felt the weight of years press on my shoulder.
Detached and still, I waited while the Others
  Passed in their endless line, the self-same road,
  Uncertain, stumbling, driven by the goad
Of goalless going . . . Clan of the Hopeless Brothers.

"Give bread," they cried. "Give bread. We starve. We perish."
  And I had but a tarnished dream to share . . .
  A lost last coin. *Misplaced* . . . not lost. Somewhere . . .
From squandered wealth a salvaged coin to cherish.
"Dreams are not bread," I thought, "Dreams are but wishes."
  Yet I had fed on dreams . . . and feasted well.
  And One before, as ancient stories tell,
Had turned a splendid dream . . . to loaves and fishes.

The Dream . . . The Deathless Light. How could I blunder?
  Food to the heart's stark hunger and despair.
  Feed, Hungry Hearts! God-given bread . . . the Wonder!
Lost in hoarding. Found . . . when sought to share.

TRIPLETS

Joy, Wonder and *God-awareness* are Siamese Triplets of our Emotional Family. They are three variants or extensions-into-expression of the one greatest emotion or force, Awareness.

At the crest of intensified Awareness, in wonder and joy, we undergo the "little death" of Personal Self. At that time we do not feel that we are *enjoying something,* we *are* the artesian out-flowing emotion itself.

We *are* Joy-full, or Joy-filled-and-overflowing from internal pressure.

We feel wonderful, wonder-full, and we are filled-and-overflowing with Wonder.

At such moments, with John Ego Adamsmith's insistent and clamorous humanness dissolved in Joy and Wonder, we are most acutely aware of God-Consciousness. The invisible plastic walls of our Sense-of-Separateness are dissolved and we consciously or subconsciously *know* our Oneness with Universe.

As Uncle Cletus used to say regarding swimming, *"Submit yo' self TO THE ELEMENT if'en you wants to swim."*

As we *"submit ourselves to the elemental awareness"* we are truly *Joy-full* and *Wonder-full.*

When Joy and Wonder are packaged in words of expression they become Appreciation, which is a less intense Awareness. It has moved up into the Intellect, or down into the Intellect.

Giving immediate articulateness to Joy or Wonder in any expression is a bit like trying to fill a gas tank while syphoning off the gas at the same time. A few creative artists, under the intense drive of awareness, produce inspired works, but for the non-creative person it is better to "hold the moment" until its radio-active energy has permeated himself.

We are admonished again and again to "Be still . . . and know."

To "know" is to "be" and to "become."

No thing, place nor person can "make" us Joy-full, but they can call forth the artesian flow from within in response to the challenge of the moment or the event.

The faucet releases the flow of water but the water comes from the vast reservoir.

You might say, *"Hawaii makes you happy when you're there."* No, it is like the open blossom of the cup-of-gold vine. It calls to be filled with the Joy-of-Living, but that Joy has been diluted with many inner tears during the years. Hawaii is only the Waiting Cup. I drink the draught that I myself have poured.

WHERE IS THE ROSE?

Where is the rose? The lens that serve our eyes
Focus events in time-space, kodak-wise,
Upon the nerves responsive to the light
In some strange process we have labeled "sight."
    And other nerves report the warm intense
    Feeling of "perfume" to the alerted sense.
    While fingertips find in the petal-curves
    Messages for telegraphing nerves.
We give the redness meanings of our own,
Memories of rouged soft lips that we have known,
Memories of romance in a summer night,
Memories of pulsant blood and Love's delight,
Memories of vows that faded, petal-wise,
Bringing sweet-bitterness of tears into our eyes.
    But somehow, somewhere in our heart there grows
    That thing of crimson Joy we call a *"rose."*

We are told that we have Five Senses. In the Idiom of Joy-Age we have only One Sense, Awareness, with the five recognized extensions-into-experience serving the One Sense, and many others of more delicate perceptions which constantly serve the one Awareness.

With our Five Senses we perceive that which we call a tree. But the "tree-ness of the tree" is known by the more subtle sense. The Greeks sensed *living spirits of growing things* and symbolized them as dryads, nymphs, fauns, satyrs. We know that this *immaterial but real* (to quote Stromberg's "Soul of the Universe") governing and organizing force is the real tree, just as the *immaterial but real Veritable Self* is the *true Self of ourselves.* Choose that name which is comfortable to your mind, but try to *"experience the tree," "experience the rose"* consciously.

Consider the lily. Consider: *"To fix the mind on; to meditate on; to bear in mind."* To *observe* with the senses, *think about* with the intellect, but to *"hold the essential, the essence, the real, the experience of the thing,"* and release the tangible as the transitory and changeful thing that it is. Where is the "real rose" after the petals have withered to dust?

WHAT'S IN A NAME? OFTEN, A FIGHT

A Frenchman and an American were sitting at a sidewalk café. A small four-legged creature with wagging tail, pleading eyes and persuasive bark sat up and begged for morsels.

"Ah, the so-charming little animal," said the Frenchman. "It is curious, however. In America you call it *'dog.'* In France we call it *'chien.'* But, of course, we both mean *'chien.'*"

"Oh, no. We both mean 'dog,'" said the American.

And the fight was on. And no one fed Fido.

**** **** **** ****

Words can be a bridge of understanding or a quicksand of confusion. Because of the encrustation of connotations and associations which are either disagreeable or unacceptable to the contemporary mind, the words, *"spiritual, religion, God, Jesus, Heaven, Christ, Divine Love,"* etc., close the mind's door for many searchers.

The words have been thundered, bleated, used as sucker-bait by charlatans, or bludgeons by the patriarchal type of father who used God's authority for getting his own way. They have been rendered sticky-sweet by the dilettantes of the Search, or they have been spoken in parrot-rote until their meaning is lost to the listener.

Yet modern science is finding that the Ancients knew intuitively what the laboratory, the telescopes, microscopes and test-tubes are confirming. *That which is called "matter" is energy at the point of perception by the five senses.*

If we had either microscopic or telescopic lens for our eyes we would see our "world" differently, and so we would regard askance the reports of another human who alone had what we now accept as human vision.

Many groups of Searchers think that they disagree, when actually they are only disagreeing over terms used. Physics says "chien"; religion "dog."

The name does not change the thing, since the name is not the thing, but only a verbal packaging for the idea.

A little Hindu tight-rope walker performs wonders on a tight-rope by working with the laws of gravity, yet he does not know it is "gravity." Yet he *knows* the laws of gravity while the physicist knows *about* gravity. I doubt whether Einstein could walk a tight-rope.

I was reared on the idea of God as a sort of Absentee Landlord who opened a subdivision called "Earth" which he leased to Man at a terrible price of pain, confusion, damnation and death. Despite all of the talk of "Love" he seemed a very unlovable and unjust and unpredictable person.

The word "Father" had little meaning to me because I early learned that my own father, while a very fine, upright man, was certainly not infallible, all-wise, nor always just, since he had human weaknesses of temper, vanities, vulnerabilities. There was a remote affection but practically no understanding between us, so the name "Father" as applied to the idea of "God" only made the whole idea more unacceptable, try as I might to believe.

In my searching I found terms which were more comfortable to my mind, "Universal Consciousness," "The One," etc.

As understanding increased I found that the substitute terms were only temporary stepladders to the climb toward understanding. Now the words "God, Christ, spiritual, etc.," are the ones I think and *feel*. The *feeling* is the important part because mere intellectual acceptance of the idea of God-Consciousness is like the intellectual acceptance of the idea that there is water.

When we thirst we want the experience of water. When we live we want the experience of God-Consciousness and God-Life, God-Presence.

The tricky word is *"and."* So long as we have the idea of God-AND-Man we are likely to have the *feeling* of separation, of duality. *"And"* places an almost imperceptible but real cellophane veil between us and the immediacy of our existence wholly in God-Consciousness. Until we have the "feeling," the realization of complete existence in God-Consciousness we are separate entities appealing to a long-distance God, and we are inclined to doubt whether our appeals can reach One who has so many sparrows to watch in their fallings.

For me, the terms Veritable Self, Veritable Consciousness, Christ-Consciousness, Mind that was in Christ-Jesus and similar terms are synonymous. At one time one of the terms will give me the feeling of "within-ness"; that is, that I am within It and It is within me. At other times another term serves. The important thing is the "feeling," the realization, the experience.

GIFT-WRAPPINGS

You and I, as John Ego Adamsmith or Jane Ego Evesmith, may love each other for years, and say, *"We know each other so well that we are like one person."* Do we? Rarely.

If we know each other only humanly, it is as though we loved a fine gift, yet had never taken off the gift-wrappings. We know that the gift inside is a fine one, but until we have truly seen it we are loving only the gift wrapping, with its *promise* of treasure within.

I have a friend whom I knew for twenty years. I thought that I knew him as well as I knew myself. My ignorance of us both was revealed when in a crisis I saw a splendid self revealed in him which was unknown to either of us. The *Veritable Self* of him came forth to meet the situation, and we were both awed and amazed at the revelation.

For me, this is not a separate Self, a separate Entity like a Guardian Angel, although it acts like one.

The word "Part" is a treacherous word for thinking because it implies "apart," as well.

In Micronesia, when our ship voyaged from Yap to Saipan to Guam to Majuro, it seemed that each island or atoll was a separate thing. But a knowledge of the formations, even limited as it is, showed that the separation was only visual. The visible part of each island or atoll was only a small fraction of the structure. Beneath the sea were vast foundations of the islands. And these foundations were all one in their base . . . Earth.

We speak of our United States as though they were really separate things. It is a man-made division. There are areas with distinctive characteristics, but all one, actually. Our continents are separate only in emergence above the sea. They are all one Earth with emergent areas.

So with John Ego Adamsmith and Jane Ego Evesmith. Only in our humanness do we seem separate. In our Seeming Selves we are apart. In our Veritable Selves, or that area-of-consciousness where the individual emerges into experience from the One Consciousness of the Universe, God, we are One. If I know myself, my Veritable Self, then I can "love you, in your Veritable Self, as my self."

In this lies our Onehood. In this our Universal Brotherhood.

With our focus-of-awareness in John Ego Adamsmith and Jane Ego Evesmith, there will always be the barrier of seeming-separateness.

There lie our Loneliness and Aloneness.

GROWTH

I found a sprouting seed with the shell burst open. We do not know for sure how much a plant feels. Creative Consciousness is the life, the substance and being of all tangible form. I believe that the sprouting seed feels pain in its own way as it becomes emergent, and the life impulse changes from static to dynamic.

I was a very long time growing up. . . .
    (Oh, I was tall, quite young. I shaved. I voted.)
But in the dog remained the wag-tail pup.
    Twenty and thirty years were lived and noted.
The tides of living carried me afar.
    I knew the flotsam and the jetsam well.
I knew the blackened cinder and . . . the star.
    Heaven was not so different from Hell.

When Youth-time passed I could not truly say;
    One night I youngly slept . . . and on the morrow
Awakened, sensing that the waiting day
    Held treasure . . . wrapped in packagings of sorrow.
Sorrow that splits the heart-seed's stubborn shell;
    Sorrow that brings the frost, the winter's wraith,
Sorrow, Gethsemane, the somber knell,
    Withering Summer's mirth . . . ripening Faith.

Sorrow . . . the night . . . without this labor-pain,
No dawn to birth the heart to Youth again.

TIMES OF FOG

There are *times of fog* that come to us
   When all familiar landmarks blur and dim.
   Our searching eyes are victims of the whim
Of clouds and mist. The stars turn traitorous
And go to hiding. Fear comes like a thief
   To steal the guiding compass of our Faith.
   The trusted Beacon changes to a wraith
Of ghost-fire, drifting like a burning leaf.
Our hearts are chilled by dark and nameless grief.

We call in vain. No echo radars back
   Assurance of some Haven in the night;
   We feel the strangling fingers of stark fright
Clutching our throats. The stiffened spine goes slack.
We know the dark night of the groping soul.
   "Where . . . where art Thou, oh, God? Oh, Father, why
   Hast thou forsaken me?" The ancient cry.
Listen. The sound of distant bells that toll . . .
"There is a Way. There is a shining Goal."
Listen. The promise in the bells that toll . . .
"There is a Way. There is a shining Goal."

**** **** **** ****

Times of Fog or periods in which "contact" is blurred or lost are recorded by the great Mystics of all faiths. Creative people know that inspiration is fluctuant. Performers have periods when music, gestures and lines "come through without static." Sometimes their production is dry, lifeless. They know their lines, music and instruments, but the artesian flow is clogged, often by tenseness, anxiety or strain.

The admonition has been given, Be still and let the *"knowing"* come through, filtered of John Ego Adamsmith's faulty human thinking or Romeo Lancelot Hamm's ego-strivings. We use the phrase *"Something*

→

seemed to tell me to do thus-and-so." Something does tell us. It is our Veritable Self, Silent Partner, Christ-Consciousness . . . call it what you will, but *recognize it and listen to it.*

Often Romeo Lancelot Hamm will masquerade as this voice. We need a great honesty with ourselves. Don't let us kid ourselves by listening to him.

"Surrender," in the human sense, has cowardly connotations. But surrender of John Ego Adamsmith or Romeo Lancelot Hamm to the Veritable Self is not cowardly. Once this has been achieved we are as unwilling to resume the garments of John Ego Adamsmith or Romeo Lancelot Hamm as to put on sweaty garments after a cleansing bath.

GREASE-PAINT

The "make-up artist" in the Movie Studios uses grease-paint, nose-putty, crêpe hair, wigs, liners, rouge, powder and lipstick to built up a Dracula, Rip Van Winkle, Hamlet or Frankenstein on the face of an actor. From the time we are born our parents, relatives, teachers, friends, enemies, books and associations are "putting on make-up" over the true face of our Veritable Self.

Strong natures are like the actors who insist upon "making up their own faces." Most of us accept these imposed lines, characteristics and prejudices or preferences, and are unaware that they are "false faces."

After the show the actor removes the make-up with cold cream, towels and vigorous cleaning. We can "remove" John Ego Adamsmith and Romeo Lancelot Hamm by spiritual cleansing until we get down to the Veritable Self, by shifting our focus-of-awareness, by meditation and the "prayer-of-listening."

A DREAM DREAMS A DREAM

When John Ego Adamsmith dreams either nightmares or pleasant dreams he is a "dream dreaming a dream." With our focus-of-awareness in our Veritable Self we see John Ego Adamsmith's life, which he perceives with senses and intellect, is as much and as little a dream as the night dreams. Events in time-space are reported by the senses. The intellect interprets or misinterprets these events. But the "interpretation" is faulty, limited, and is a dream or a nightmare according to interpretation.

DEEPER THAN THE WORD

There is communion deeper than the word,
More intimate . . . the poetry unheard,
The swift-flashed look, the touch, the warm caress,
Conveying messages of tenderness.
   Life has so much to tell which it must tell
   In silence; words dilute the magic spell
   Of Intuition's subtle swift exchange,
   Soft nuances of feeling past the range
   Of *words, words, words,* those packagings of thought
   That rattle like crisp popcorn sacks when taut
   Receptive nerves are waiting to respond
   To Beauty pulsing in from the Beyond.

The Heart is like a film exposed to light,
Sensitized to values, dark and bright,
To shades of gray, the fugitive and sky,
Evading capture by the seeking eye.
   So, go in stillness to the rendezvous
   With Beauty, listen . . . she will speak to you
   In wordless speech. Accept what you have heard
   And do not limit it by thought or spoken word.
Joy is artesian, pulsing, surging, flowing up.
Put lips to the Heart's red curve . . . it's only Cup.

It is hard to still the random and irrelevant thoughts which run around
barefoot, like mischievous urchins, in our minds. Let them alone, those
urchin thoughts. They will snooze in due time.

Rest easy. Gently draw the focus-of-awareness higher and higher, out
of the circling valley of the limited senses, away from the intellectual
horizontals of the plains, to the high clean places of the peaks where
released horizons give the eagle-heart limitless sky for flight.

THREE CITIES

Pleasure is of the senses; happiness of the heart, but Joy, in the Idiom of Joy-
Age . . . listen to the legend of The Three Cities.

There were three ancient cities; one that stood
   Against the desert's edge, one on the plains
   And one among the hills. The seasons' rains
Made green the grass and fields and shady wood
Of that fair gardened city, rich with treasure,
   Where rites of mirth and revelry came first
   In worship of the Quencher of the Thirst,
The Rain God in the *City of Bright Pleasure.*
   And when the dry winds blustered from the South
   There were deep cisterns filled against the drouth.

Beside the second city ran a stream
   Of cool clear water rushing from the hills
   To pulse in man-made veins of earth in rills
That nourished fields of grain and fed the dream
Of plenty that sustained the people's strength;
   For when drouth came to curse the neighbor land
   It spared this place the clutch of its harsh hand,
Passing above its watered breadth and length.
   The people made the stream their God, to bless,
   Naming it with a name, *"Heart's Happiness."*

The city built against the desert's edge
   Knew rain for what it was, a transient thing,
   And knew that streams can both withhold and bring
Their gifts, unbound by pleading or by pledge.
Deep in the stubborn earth the people toiled
   To find beneath the dark resistant ground
   Sources of water, hidden and profound,
Flowing in rocky arteries that coiled
   From distant peaks of primal snow to course
   In *Joy* artesian . . . constant at its Source.

A time of testing came unto the land;
  The rains withheld; the cisterned city parched.
  The streams dried up. Across the country marched
The Tyrants, Hunger, Thirst and Death, a band
Of Robber Kings, the Killer and the Thief,
  Sacking the Pleasure City of the Plains,
  Stealing from Happiness its garnered grains,
Paying with specious currencies of Grief.
  Only the City of Deep Wells withstood
  The long harsh siege of Life's Dark Brotherhood.

**** **** **** ****

ARTESIAN . . . SPONTANEOUS . . . FOUNTAIN

ARTESIAN WELL: a well made by *boring into the earth* till *water is reached* which, from *internal pressure, flows spontaneously* like a *fountain.*
  SPONTANEOUS: proceeding from, or acting by, *internal impulse, energy or natural law, without external force,* as spontaneous *flow.*
  FOUNTAIN: a spring of water issuing from the earth, the source or the head, as of a river.
THE WELL OF JOY: a well made by boring through the shallow surface soil of Pleasure and external appearances, and through the firmer but human soil of Happiness or emotions, prejudices and opinions, to that depth which, from internal pressure of the eternally out-flowing Power of the Presence there, flows spontaneously like a fountain, the inexhaustible artesian joyousness which is our heritage.

OIL MILLIONAIRES

My people owned a bit of Oklahoma land which would not have supported a pair of dieting prairie dogs. They sold it. The next owners dug and struck oil. They became Oil Millionaires. We had been Oil Millionaires without the use of our Millions because we were *unaware* of the oil beneath our land.
Dig and strike your gusher of Joy. Be the Joy Millionaire that you *are.*
  And spend it, Brother, spend it!

JOY KNOWS THE FACE OF GRIEF

Because I sing of Joy, my Cynic Friend,
  Don't be deceived, I know the face of Grief;
  The snail of Doubt has slimed the greening leaf
Of Faith, oh, often! I have had to bend
Before Fear's dreadful winds; the hurricanes
  Of War have thrice thrown down the Citadel
  Which I had built from broken stones. Full well
My Heart knows Disillusionment's dull pains.

Because I know the bleak white skull of Death
  Lies underneath the flesh that I caress,
  I love the more, and with more tenderness.
The Power that *gives* . . . and *takes* the transient breath
Is greater than the moment's Grief or Bliss.
  The Pattern on the Loom is far too vast
  For children's eyes to see; the shadow cast
By Night is but Tomorrow's chrysalis.

For reasons far beyond my human ken
  The Rose *must* bloom despite the blighting Snail;
  The Oak *must* stand against the testing Gale.
And Faith must bloom through Drouth's in Hearts of Men.
My proof would not be proof to you. Belief
  Seems fragile shield against the Cynic's thrust,
  And yet, my Heart in stainless steel of Trust
Cries "Joy" before the Battlements of Grief.

NOT THERE

"Not *there* will you find Joy," He said, "not *there*."
The firefly's quick lamp is not a star.
Nor is the star the beacon light afar.
Even the sun is not the guiding flare.
Be *still*, Child, hush the pantings of desire;
  The rain of tears, the smoke and fogs of shame
  May veil but never quench Joy's white clear flame.
  Curve your cupped hands to shield the inward gaze
  And look . . . look with young eyes of bright amaze . . .
Within your heart burns the luminous Fire.

"AS"

I see God . . . standing *as* the tree,
And feel God-life . . . *as* all of me.
The tree, myself, the sun, the clod . . .
What *could* we be but Word of God
Made flesh, as light, *as* earth, *as* wood;
One Life in one vast Fatherland,
Expressing seed and sperm and earth
In *multi-form* and *multi-birth.*

The tree, myself, the earth, the sun,
Light, flesh and wood . . . yet *always One,*
Why can not you and I and tree
Know *God as us* . . . and *us* as *"We?"*

Again we have the message of the Considered Lily which says: "Can you not *see* and *know* that, although we are individual in form, activity and purpose, we are the One Conscious Creative Life and Power and Consciousness *experiencing itself* through expression as us, as the tiniest and the mightiest, the tangible and the intangible? Dissolve the plastic illusion of Personal Self into the Immaterial but Real *Veritable Self,* and feel and know that mighty Oneness. That is *Joy.*"

Many people have asked for a sequel to the Scarecrow Romance of Windy Willie and Calico Ann from my book, "A Grand Time Living." Like children, they insisted, "What happened next? Tell us some more." So here is "more."

SCARECROW WALTZ

Windy Willie and Calico Ann,
Scarecrow Spinster and Scarecrow Man,
Lived their tatter-rag wind-blown days
Staring with lovelorn hopeless gaze
Across the space where a cruel barbed wire
Fenced them off from their deep desire
To live and love in the romanced way
Of humans they watched by night and day.
   They looked with a yearning, stark and vain,
   At night when the lights in the window-pane
   Of the farmhouse near showed silhouettes
   Of local Romeo-Juliets
   Flirting and fussing and making up
   In the way of men since Time was a pup.
The scarecrows longed for the spark-divine
To burn in *their* hearts of pine and twine.
Their arms of sticks would almost ache
(if wood *could* ache) to somehow make
Those loving gestures, the soft embrace
And feel a smile on a corn-husk face.
They never *quite* ceased to hope and pray
That love would *somehow* find a way.
   Hopes and prayers are curious things;
   They *sometimes* pull those cosmic strings
   Which some call Fate and some call Chance,
   To make Life's pitiful puppets dance.
One night . . . the stars in a certain sign
Traced lines of light in a strange design;
Made a mystic mood pervade the Earth
And the air was filled with a Cosmic Mirth;
Flowers that only bloomed by day
Opened their petals in a reckless way.

Grandfather-clocks struck seventy chimes
And school bells tolled in jitterbug times;
Roosters crowed as though it was dawn
And hens laid eggs on the green front lawn.
    The Wind who was Friend of the scarecrow pair,
    Sang a raffish song with a witching air,
    With a *Tra-la-la* and a *Whoopsy-doo*
    That stirred the scarecrows through and through.
    They felt a tingling, strange and thrilling,
    And the throb of a pulse-beat flooding, filling
    Their dusty bodies of twine and pine . . .
    The *heat* and *flame* of that *spark-divine!*
They *couldn't* believe that it *could be true.*
They ventured a hesitant step or two
Then, light as leaves in the circling air,
They leaped from the ground, this Fabulous Pair,
And *met* and *mingled* in rapturous bliss
And *knew the thrill of their first dazed kiss.*

        The Wind brushed a tear from his vaporous eye
        To hear Will laugh and Annie cry.
        All night long the Wind played tunes,
        Mad as the crying of moonstruck loons,
        Waltzes, two-steps, gay gavottes,
        Cake-Walks, schottisches, jigs and trots,
        High-jinks, low-jinks, Highland flings,
        And nameless frivolous posturings,
        Dancing, prancing in blissful pleasure . . .
        The scarecrows *never missed a measure.*
The sun at dawn heard the beat and thrill
And hustled daylight over the hill
To see the show . . . but all he found
Was *a heap of sticks* on the frosty ground,
With a rag or two and some tattered papers
To mark the scene of the madcap capers.

A hobo wandering by at dusk
Found some twigs and a dry corn-husk
To make a fire to cook his stew
In an old tin can as hobos do.
He piled the twigs on the rags and sticks,
But the fire he made played curious tricks.
And the skin of his neck began to creep
As the flames curled up to lick and leap,
   For he heard strange laughter and puckish squeals,
   And the smoke rolled up in *Virginia Reels,*
   And he heard a pipe piping a tune,
   And saw ghosts dancing a rigadoon.
Round and round in a giddy swirl,
A raggedy man and a slim gay girl,
Bow and curtsy, smile and flirt,
With tapping feet and a flouncing skirt,
Over the fence and over the field,
While the pipes of the wind-flute skirled and pealed.
    All through the dusk and a long time after
    Came the sound of the gay far laughter,
    From the place where the Scarecrow Girl and Man
    Dance forever to Pipes of Pan.

Is it only a dream? Could the tale be true?
In the heart of me and the heart of you
There's a wind-song, wistfully gay and silly,
And a Calico Ann and a Windy Willie.

Why do fairy tales hold such immemorial appeal to people? Because children in their simplicity, and our Veritable Selves in their wisdom, know that that's the way life should be, Happy Ending, Happy Beginning . . . and a Happy Always.

SPLENDID LAUGHTER

I saw curtains of orchids, pendant from towering trees,
draping a jungle-glade in Guatemala
near the ancient ruins of the Lost City of Quirigua.
Butterflies with jeweled satin wings
stitched vanishing patterns of beauty on the petal-brocades
in this boudoir of some fabulous Moon-Queen.
    I swam for hours in the peacock-blue lagoon of Majuro
    in the Islands Beyond Yesterday, Micronesia,
    above mermaids' gardens where creations in coral, fin and scale
    were more fantastic than the maddest whimsies
    of a delirious French milliner
    or a genius-jeweler commissioned to make the gauds
    for Amphitrite of the Green Hair.
I followed a vagrant trail in the Oregon Cascade mountains
where all of the raspberry, strawberry and pineapple sherbet
in the world seemed to be spilled for the delectation of children
with insatiable appetites and unlimited capacity. . . .
    The azaleas and rhododendron were in bloom.
Silent Partner, who knows all of my thoughts, chuckled at me . . .
*"You are thinking that it's a pity that year after year
all of this beauty is wasted with no one to see and enjoy it."*
    It is not wasted.
    It is the greatest delight of Creative God
    to think Beauty into Form . . .
When you are in the gray quiet of your room at twilight,
or when a melancholy for dead beauty comes upon you,
remember, oh, remember that *only the form changes.*
Beauty is immortal. Beauty is ever renewed
for it is Creative God's robust and splendid laughter.
    Rejoice and enjoy. Live in-joy.
        Joy!

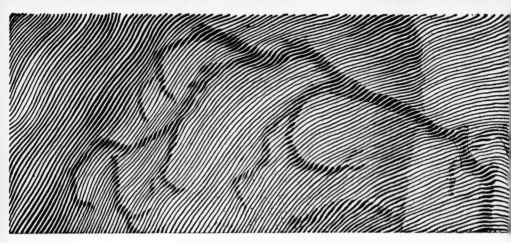

CLOSED FOR THE SEASON

The tattered telegrams of autumn leaves
Delivered by the Wind in drifting sheaves
Bring messages that cause quick consternation
To summer-folks, the roses. "End Vacation."
Leaf-salads that supplied the brown fawn's needs
Are now replaced by cereals of seeds.
Along the road a thousand road-signs tell . . .
"Closed for the Winter . . . Nature's green Motel."

ETERNAL TRIANGLE

Marriage, my Dear, is a Triangle . . .
YOUR-angle, OUR-angle, MY-angle.
And the usual cause when we *do* wrangle
Is the question of I-US-or-YOU-angle.
I object when you say that the sure angle
Of OUR-angle ought to be YOUR-angle,
When I KNOW that a RIGHT-ANGLE-triangle
MUST be based on a *right*-angle . . . MY-angle.
(and then the fight began)

ARGUMENT AMONG THE FLORA
LOTUS, CACTUS AND AIR-PLANT

Lotus, Cactus and Air-Plant were arguing about the best place to live.
"Of course, the Pool is the *only* place to live," said Lotus.
"My roots are in the black, cool nutritious mud.
I never have to worry about water. I live in water.
My Lover, the Sun, beckons me through the cool translucent depths.
I rise effortlessly to the surface to that joyous rendezvous.
The Pool is the *only* place to live."
  "Mud, ugh!" said Cactus. "How revolting.
My roots are in the hot, dry sand. I never worry about water.
That's what makes you the soft fragile thing you are, Lotus,
your dependence on that thin wet stuff. I thrive on drouth.
The desert is the *only* place to live."
"How silly you both are," said Air-Plant.
"I don't root in *anything*.
The wind brings me my food.
The dew is my drink.
I'm a free soul."
The Spirit of All Green Growing Things said to them,
"Foolish Children. You are all rooted in Life.
Each to his own soil."

**** **** **** ****

* If you ask me, "What books would you recommend for the Joyous Journey?" I could say only this: "Once you have started sincerely on the Search, and *are alerted for Road-Signs and Patrin,* you will find books, pages, paragraphs and lines coming almost magically to your attention, *when you trust the guidance of your Veritable Self.*" I can say with the Spirit of All Green Growing Things, "You are rooted in God-Consciousness. Draw sustenance from that Source. Your needs will be met."
  "Ask and ye shall receive" is not an idle statement.
    Listen, and you will hear.

* See pages 55–124 for suggestions.

UNFINISHED AUTOBIOGRAPHY

In The South Seas

Why do I feel poor in this Summer Land?
  Between my fingers runs the golden chain
Of jewel-days, unflawed. Quick to my hand
  Are Midas-riches. Prisms of the rain
Build opal arches on the sky by day
  And moonstone arches on the sabled night;
Even the sands are gold. A King's display
  Wearies the eye with treasure and delight.

How can I hunger where there is no need,
  No sense unsated, no wish unfulfilled?
The Cup of Pleasure, drained in reckless speed,
  Brims as it empties, prodigally spilled.
Why does an aching silence pain my ears
  As music stirs the air with rhythmic beat,
The drums of passion, tinkling chandeliers
  Of tropic stars like wind-harps, sharply sweet?

Why am I not content? Why hunger-cursed
  When all that I have sought I have . . . and more?
The bouquet of the wine is in the thirst
  After the goblet crashes to the floor.
Hunger is sauce to give the feast its zest,
  Silence is obbligato to the song.
Spring is born of the frost in Autumn's breast.
  Time without waiting, wanting, lingers long.

I need gray days as prelude to the sun.
   The search for bread reveals the taste of bread,
Grainy and golden. When the day is done
   Night's dark sad trumpets hail the dawn ahead.
Satiety, not leavings of the swine,
   Are husks that urge the Prodigal's return.
"Thy kindly-cruel will be done . . . not mine."
   Why does it take so long . . . so long, to learn?

TIGHT-ROPE OVER GRAND CANYON

Learning to keep our focus-of-awareness out of John Ego Adamsmith's limited and obstructed False-Consciousness and to keep it constantly in the Veritable Consciousness is like learning to walk again after an adult illness or learning to walk across Grand Canyon on a tight-rope.
   It is a matter of practice, persistence . . . and confidence.
   Confidence that it *can be done,* preceding the attempt.
   Persistence growing from the confidence-without-proof.
   Practice to achieve perfection in dexterity of action.
Walking is a matter of losing and regaining balance. Step-fall-balance. Step-fall-balance. Walking a tight-rope is a highly developed extension of this ability.
   Yet the tight-rope walker with his practiced skill
   can perform feats of balance on the thin swaying rope
   which we can not equal in our clumsy amateurishness
   on flat ground.
The convalescent may use crutches or a cane for a while. The tight-rope walker will use his balancing pole. The seeker for Veritable Consciousness will use books, statements of Truth, instructors and guides. In time these may all be put aside.
   The Walker walks with unconscious attention to balance,
   but if he neglects this alerted unconscious awareness
   he falls. Then he says, "Oops, sorry!" And tries, and *walks* again.

The tight-rope walker's attention shifts to a beckoning blonde
below. For an interval he is flapping and tensing to regain the
lost balance.

The Seeker slips back into habit-reflexes of the race and the personality of John Ego Adamsmith or Romeo Lancelot Hamm . . .
and goes *boom!* He says, "Oops, sorry!" And tries . . . and walks
. . . again.

The tight-rope walker becomes integrated
with his conscious and unconscious sense of balance
so that he can walk a tight-rope across Grand Canyon
and yet enjoy and include the grandeur of the scene.

The Walker progresses from stumbling to walking confidently.
He runs, leaps, performs acrobatics and possibly progresses
to tight-rope walking . . . through practice, persistence and
confidence. If he becomes overconfident and forgetful he
loses his balance . . . and . . . starts again.

Of course, the rule, "the higher the farther the fall," holds
good here. As we gain "spiritual dexterity in walking the
tight-rope over the abyss" our falls are more severe in impact. But, fortunately, "gravity" does not remember our sins
against it when we regain our balance. It works *with*
us always. Spiritual "gravity" is equally forgiving. That
is our good fortune. It is the story of the Prodigal's
fatted calf and gold ring. It is the theme of the poem
Eleventh Hour, page 132.

To "sin" is to miss the mark. "Evil" is the wrong way of doing things.
When we "sin" against gravity we fall. Gravity does not punish us. We
punish ourselves.

We can neither make nor break laws.
We break ourselves against the immutable laws.
They are for our use and protection.
Seeming miracles are performed by working with the laws.
True miracles are merely results of working with laws of
which we generally have little knowledge.

The words "natural" and "supernatural" should be reversed in meaning.
The spiritual or supernatural is the normal and natural in the eyes
of the Veritable Self. Only John Ego Adamsmith, with his focus-of-
awareness in his senses and intellect, regards them as miracles.

Continued from page 55.

and in the splendid concluding chapters read what that inspired physicist has to say about the inability of the *"rabble of the senses and the arrogant intellect"* to comprehend the causes behind appearances. He would be combing nebulae and comets out of his hair for the rest of his life.

He would find *"The Soul of the Universe"* by Gustaf Stromberg and learn of the Organizing Field, immaterial but real, and never thereafter regard a seed or an egg or a cocoon without tingling awe and wonder.

I would say to the young G.I.: "I can say of these books only this; *each for me was a splendid Patrin, each guiding in its own way, to the understanding of Joy-Age. Your Tumbleweed Heart will find its own soil."*

The Troward Lectures with scholarly and illuminating pages. *Sermon on the Mount,* by Emmet Fox, which was the first patrin I found, apparently casually, when I began my earnest search. *This Thing Called Life & This Thing Called You* by Ernest Holmes. Dr. Holmes encouraged my work along these lines and made available his many groups to "try out" my material and to learn in trying. *The Infinite Way* and other writings by Joel Goldsmith. As student and as friend I am grateful to Joel Goldsmith for hours of inspiring talk and splendid instruction. *Letters of the Scattered Brotherhood* by Mary Strong; balm to a weary heart and cool water for those who thirst. *The Search for God* by Marchette Chute, clarifying much which is obscure in the Old Testament. *The Conquest of Fear* by Basil King, a simple powerful statement. *Dr. Suzuki's writing on Zen;* wisdom of the East as catalyst for much of the inspiration of the West. The Upanishads and the Baghavad Gita. *Change Your Life Through Prayer* by Stella Terrill Mann, as practical as a darning-needle *silver-plated with star-dust. King James Version of the Bible,* and *any or all* contemporary versions for idiom of our age. Any writings related to Mahatma Gandhi. *The Wisdom of Insecurity* by Allan Watts. *Cosmic Consciousness* by Bucke. The Poems of *Walt Whitman.* The Writings of *Emerson.* The writings of *Kahlil Gibran. Creation Continues* by Fritz Kunkel. Somewhere among these and others he might pick up the thread which would lead him on to his own Journey.

Many writers, speakers and people in general until recently brought the word "God" into the conversation apologetically or by the side-door, like a rich eccentric relative who must be included but not featured in Family Gatherings. The reverse is the order today.

The young G.I. (or you, if you are a beginner on the Journey) might ask, *"Are there schools, organizations, churches and movements where I might find this Way taught?"*

Yes. Many. One of the all-utility names for this pattern of thought is *"New Thought,"* but I would call it *Re-newed Thought* because the basic teachings were old when Jesus detonated the greatest spiritual atomic-bomb which ever shattered an old world of thought and made way for the new.

Truth was never new. It has always been . . . since the beginningless beginning. But recognition and re-recognition of Truth, in various packagings, has gone on through the centuries.

Mary Baker Eddy was one of the greatest of the contemporary voices to voice again the ancient truths. Since her time many voices have been lifted with variations of the basic teachings, that Man is inseparable from God-Consciousness *except through his misconception in human thinking. Each Seeker on the Journey will find the Road congenial to him.*

I can not hope to do more than sketch and suggest this vast subject on which thousands of books have been written. I am neither teacher nor preacher. But, if I can be an "infecter," I hope I will have done my part.

Here's a condensation of what I feel about it. You and I are John Ego Adamsmith living pretty much in our senses and intellects, such as they are. With our eyes we look at *surfaces,* since eyes are constructed that way. With our intellects we think *about things.* But we *know* and *experience* life with our Veritable Consciousness.

The human intellect demands that there must have been *some sort of beginning.* Then it promptly asks, *"But what came before that?"*

We are handicapped. We can't see *what we are* because *we are what we are.* We can't see into our own eyes with our own eyes. We can't even see our own faces. We see only photographs, reflections . . . and the tips of our noses.

Because of our habits of thinking, the name "God" which should be a key to understanding may be a plastic wall through which we can not reach.

We use the name "God" as a noun. A "noun" is the *name* of a *thing.* GOD is *no thing* yet all things were made *by* and *of* God, and without Creative God-Consciousness was not any thing made that was made.

The senses and intellect, dealing largely with tangibles, protest, *"But something can't come out of nothing."* And that is true.

Maybe this will help. Modern physics says that matter is only energy at the point of perception by our senses. With telescopic or microscopic or X-ray lens in our eyes we'd "see" the world differently, therefore it would "be" different, so far as we are concerned. The word "real" would have different meanings. A man with our "normal" vision who visited a land of microscopic-telescopic-X-ray lensed people would be disbelieved when he described the world as we "see" it.

"Things" are only Creative Consciousness, individualized, experiencing itself in form and activity. The One Creative Consciousness, *in* which and *as* which we live, move and have our being, is all there is, and to quote Ethel Barrymore's famous line, *"that's all there is . . . there isn't any more."*

There is no conflict between Modern Science and the Ancient Truths, except the difference in language and terms. Read "What's in a Name?" on page 100.

**** **** **** ****

I'd tell the young G.I. *"I feel as though I'm trying to knit a sweater out of fog and cigarette smoke* because words are just air under pressure, vibrating stretched cords, *but still I'm trying."*

In the Beginningless Beginning (which is beyond our comprehension, humanly) there was That which is the Eternal Now. There is no more and there's no less "Universe" now than there was in the Beginmingless Beginning, because all that *was* and all that *is* and all that *ever will be* is the One Creative Consciousness, God, *realizing* and *expressing* and *experiencing* itself in all created form *as* all life and *as* all consciousness.

The young G.I. (or you) might ask, *"But how do we use all of this in achieving a joyous life in a world where so many aspects are un-joyous, terrifying and hopeless?"*

I could say only what I say to myself hourly, "By the same method by which I would become a doctor, singer, artist or craftsman of any kind . . . by study, practice and application of the principle of my study. It is an individual job. *It's an inside job exteriorly expressed."*

There are a few more ideas about form and substance which have helped me.

Form is only a quality of Creative Consciousness. Form has never added anything to Substance, and there is no Substance except the One Creative Consciousness, God, and "all things were made by Him, and without Him was not anything made that was made." Those are not just words; it is a statement of a principle which science will confirm more and more, only in different terms.

I'd say to the young G.I. "Maybe the word 'Him' throws you off because 'Him' makes you think of a picture of a greatly amplified Man somewhere off in Somewhere, making worlds and sparrows and men and atoms and seas and tossing them out into Somewhere Else to be Universe."

If God is All, then All means ALL, and not "All *and* something else."

Creative Consciousness is beyond "He," "She" or "It," because it contains all that is. We are conscious of ourselves only because the One Consciousness is conscious of itself in Oneness and Diversity.

You and I are each capable of saying and feeling "I am." Uncountable millions are conscious of "I am." We're not like electric machines, plugged into some central powerhouse and drawing supply from it in order to act like intelligent automatons. Where does the power come from?

Everything in the Universe is life, power and consciousness, expressing, each in its degree and quality, the awareness "Am." It may not be aware as man is of "I" and "AM," but its livingness is an expression of "AM."

Here's a little trick which helped me to realization. Take a lump of sugar and drop it into a tall glass of warm water. Watch it dissolve and disappear.

What is lost? Only *form*. All that went to make that lump-form is still there, diffused but not lost in the warm water.

Turn to page 92 and read "Rain." And then to page 58, ONE.

As long as our focus-of-awareness is centered in our seeming-selves or John Ego Adamsmith we are not realizing our Oneness with the One Consciousness. If we can dissolve the personal self into the Veritable Self, as we dissolved the lump of sugar into the water, we can get something of the "feeling" of this oneness.

The focus-of-awareness can be shifted from one area-of-consciousness to another as the beam of a flashlight can be shifted in a dark room from one area to another. It takes discipline and practice, but what doesn't that is worth achieving?

→

We will begin to realize that the human personality is merely a skin suggesting but not revealing the Veritable Self or Christ-consciousness of ourselves, just as our features suggest us but are not actually *us*.

The clamor of John Ego Adamsmith's human desires, fears and anxieties and resentments is so loud that we find it difficult to "be still and know." By being completely acquiescent we prepare ourselves, through meditation and contemplation of these ideas, for the moment when Veritable Self will reveal itself so completely that there is no longer any doubt.

The poem "Three Ears" gives a little idea of this listening. The lines are not merely poetic imagery. They state an actual experience. Hearing the "growingness of ground" is an actual ability of the Veritable Self. Oneness with Life is possible when we are aware that we, in our Inner Selves, *are* Life.

As the tip of your finger is only an extension of your body at that point where the particular activity of "touch" is experienced, and is no wise a *part apart,* so we, in our individual sense of consciousness are only the point of the One Consciousness where it is emergent into tangible experience of its own life and being. We are in no way a *part apart.*

The Consciousness of the Veritable Self is like the white beam of undifferentiated light going out from a Projection Machine in a darkened room to the silver screen. That is the Power. That is the Consciousness.

Put into it the slides of John Ego Adamsmith's human thinking. Onto the screen of his human consciousness go the pictures. He interprets them according to his temperament, background, prejudices and preferences, but he does not see the true picture.

A child or a savage would mistake the projected pictures of an actual Projection Machine for reality. If the picture is upside down the child or savage would try to turn the screen around to correct the mistake. The enlightened man would go to the Projection Machine and there "right the picture."

We do not put out the forest fire on the screen by dashing water on the picture. We remove the slide from the white beam of light.

Judge not by appearances. We can't, but we eternally try.

THE FLURRY-GO-ROUND

*I almost dread getting mail these days because it's so likely that there will be
a letter saying that an old friend, Bill, Bob, Mike, Brad or Monty has "fallen off
the Flurry-Go-Round" because he wouldn't get off in time. I know the futility of
giving advice because I so seldom take it myself . . . but I offer this bit for what
it may be worth.*

Come on, let's get off of the Flurry-Go-Round,
The Hurry-Go-Round, the Scurry-Go-Round,
The speed-driven, greed-riven, Worry-Go-Round.
   The straining and blowing . . . *and where are we going?*
   The cussing and fretting . . . *and what are we getting?*
   The huffing and puffing . . . *and can't-get-enoughing.*
   The sweating and stewing . . . *and what are we doing?*
Just going around . . . and a r o u n d . . . and a r o u n d.
Then, what will we do with whatever we've found
When we think that we're bound for six feet underground
When we finish our round on the Hurry-Go-Round,
While the Flurry-Go-Round goes around and a r o u n d
And around . . . and a r o u n d . . . and a r o u n d?
   Do we have to *fall off* of the Merry-Go-Round?
   Time will *slap us* all off of the Scary-Go-Round.
   So why not *crawl off* of the Blarey-Go-Round
And let it go 'round and a r o u n d and a r o u n d
And   a r o u n d
And   a r o u n d
And   a r o u n d !

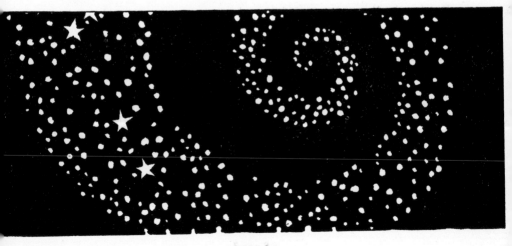

PRODIGAL DAUGHTERS . . . PRODIGAL SONS

Mrs. Lot of Biblical fame is ancestress of all Prodigal Sons and Prodigal Daughters.

Our blood-line is recognizable by the reflex of looking back on Renounced Delights which makes us stumble as we go forward to Anticipated Rewards.

We may not turn to Pillars of Salt,
But there will be enough salt tears shed
To make a Pillar as a Road-Marker
For the Two-Way Traffic
Between Babylon and Home.

After we return from our Sojourn in Babylon we know a period of great contentment.

We feel snugly and smugly secure.

We even become glib, garrulous and tiresome
With our repeated boast,
"*Babylon? Never again.*"
    This is the Dangerous Age.

After the Fatted Calf has been digested and the Gold Ring become familiar to our hand, the first fine delight stales into accustomedness.

The Wayward Wanderer is just Johnny Everyday.

Hours of idle dreaming bring memories of Unfinished Business of pleasure and gratification.

We know a sneaking regret,
Not for the things we did
But for the things we *didn't do.*
We chance upon that little red book
With names and addresses
Which we should have thrown away . . . but didn't.
We become nostalgic for the good old, bad old days . . .
And nights.

We rationalize until we sell ourselves and the more credulous home-folks on the idea that we ought to get that furniture that we left in storage (for our debts) at the Court of the Five Senses, Primrose Way, Babylon.

It's a practical idea.
We know our way home.
We've learned our lesson.
Or have we?
We were *given* our first chance. We *earn* our second chance.
　We learn the hard way.
I've often wondered why the story of the Prodigal Son fascinated me.
It was my own biography . . . written before I lived it.
　Prodigal Daughter . . . Prodigal Son,
　No rent controls in Babylon.
　　For a while it's fun.
　　When the fun is done,
　They raise the rents in Babylon.
　Rents come high in Babylon.

ETERNAL SONG

　Only the singing ends.
　　The song goes on.
　　The note released
　　Has never ceased
　　Its echoed antiphon.
　Through Time and Space it bends,
　　The old-new note,
　　Returning to some songbird's throat,
　　And reascends
　　To swell the Chorus of the Spheres
　　Through endless years.
　The song goes on . . . only the singing ends.

BABYLON, in the Idiom of Joy-Age, represents the belief that in material things, in mechanical comforts, luxuries, in places, people and wealth we will find the happiness, security and life which we believe that we want. After the spiritual vision there is often a Return to Babylon, even as the Prodigal Son, even as You and I, until we learn to enjoy without depending upon the tangibles.

FROM PRODIGAL SON'S DIARY

Babylon was glamorous when I was young.
Amorous and clamorous the sense-songs sung.
The wine was very heady. The women, ripe and sweet.
And gay mad music followed my feet.

I went back to Babylon . . . just last year.
Babylon was shabby. Babylon was drear.
Stale was the incense. Rancid were the musks.
And bitter, bitter, bitter the taste of husks.

Stubborn, contradictory, we Prodigal Sons,
Maverick and wilful, the Driven Ones.
Squandering the gold; hoarding tinsel-glitters,
Insisting that the Cup needs . . . *a dash of bitters.*

ELEVENTH HOUR

Prodigal, Prodigal, on your way home,
   On your way home through the long, gray dusk,
   Your sad eyes strain
   From the bitter drouth
   Of tears unshed;
   Hot on your mouth
   Is the telltale stain
   Of harlot-red
   And the brown stain of the husk.
     Your sick heart fears the clang of the gate,
     The harsh, cold clang of the closing gate,
      "Too late! Too late!"
Prodigal, Prodigal, on your way home
   Through the lonely dusk . . .
     It is not too late.
     Against the night,
     Beyond the gate . . .
     LIGHT!

TELL THE TALES OF BABYLON

When Prodigal Son became, in the course of years, Grandfather, he was besieged
by the youngsters with demands for Tales of Babylon.

Tell us tales of Babylon when you were there.
Was it, as they say it was, sinfully fair?
Were the temples builded of brick and brass and gold?
Were the women wanton and tempting to behold?
Babylon was splendid. Babylon was great.
But Pride was in the Temple and Death at the Gate.
Babylon is ruins now, the home of snake and owl.
People (I among them) made it foul.

Babylon had gardens hanging in the sky.
Babylon had glories to delight the eye.
Babylon was lovely for a transient while.
People (I among them) made it vile.
When the tales of cities are told and ended . . .
People made them what they were . . . vile or splendid.

FOR THE ALTAR

The Lesser Gods like frankincense and myrrh,
    Jewels and the flesh of bullocks seared with flames,
Music of flutes and rhythmed sacred dance,
    And the chanting of sonorous empty names.

Oh, God, who gives to all the all we are,
    If with bare hands I tear a crimson rift
In my own breast to take my pulsant heart
    As sacrifice . . . *is this the acceptable gift?*

IDIOM OF JOY-AGE

The *Divine Claustrophobia* is Samson
pushing back the Pillars of the False Temple
with strength which is not muscular but spiritual.
The *Tumbleweed Heart* is Columbus
seeking the Released Horizons of a New World
which intuitively he knows are there
but most prove to himself and to the world.
The *Divine Restlessness* is the young eagle
feeling the call of Space to his untried wings.
Flight is in his heart
But he must prove it through his wings.

TUMBLEWEED HEART. When the Divine Claustrophobia or spirit-ual dread of cramped spaces activates in the human consciousness it is the Veritable Self or Christ-Consciousness asserting its power in the human consciousness. *There will be no rest again in that heart.*

WHEN THE TUMBLEWEED HEART stirs to growth in John Ego Adamsmith he feels a driving restlessness which may make him seek far places of the earth or far-near places of his Inner Self.

IN THE ONE CASE he may go to the Paradises of the South Seas or to the silences of the Frozen North. But he will find that he has brought with him that which he seeks or that which he seeks to flee from which is . . . Himself.

UNTIL HE TURNS WITHIN to find his Islands Beyond Yesterday, his vagabonding will be always a mirage, retreating as he advances toward it or beckoning irresistibly if he seeks to rest or turn from the search. *"Let him turn from the seeking, and the eagle will eat his heart."*

HE MAY SEEK in any of the hundreds of philosophies, cults, ration-alizations, and temporary "cures" of psychiatry, psychology or men-tal discipline and exercises. Until he has had the *"experience of God-Consciousness"* with the realization of his inseparable oneness with the One Consciousness, he will blow with the winds of Chance and Fate like the tumbleweed of the prairies.

IDIOM OF JOY-AGE

WE ARE ISLANDS: *An island is an area of land surrounded by water.* My Micronesian voyage brought me realization and "feeling" of an idea which I had accepted intellectually but had not made a part of the living awareness of God-Consciousness as a power more definite in its immaterial reality than gravity.

AS WE CRUISED from island to island, from Guam to Yap to Saipan to Koror to Babelthaup to Majuro, we passed other islands which we saw but did not visit. There were lonely little atolls like coral ringworms on the blue skin of the Pacific, and high jungled mountainous islands draped in green brocades of forest. Each had its own characteristics and each seemed individual, a *part apart* from the others.

IN THEIR EMERGENCE ABOVE WATER they are individuals in size, climate, scenery and characteristics, as different and as alike as brothers and sisters of one family.

BUT THE BASE OF EACH, the vast submerged and invisible part of each island is inseparably joined with the One Body, Earth.

ISLANDS ARE ONLY EARTH EMERGENT above the ocean at individual points, but in no way separate or *a part apart*.

SUDDENLY THE REALIZATION CAME, with an almost sensuous awareness, that you and I and all of the other people in the world, now and through all time, are islands of individuality surrounded by a sea of appearances which, with our senses and intellect, we accept as our world, our life.

BUT ONLY IN OUR EMERGENCE are we individuals. The great submerged areas-of-consciousness in each of us are inseparably joined with the One Creative Consciousness, God.

AS JOHN EGO ADAMSMITH, with our focus-of-awareness in our senses and intellect, we seem to be individual islands. In our Veritable Selves we are one with the Oneness. In the realization of that idea comes our vision of the Land of Joy-Age, the Kingdom of Heaven which is within.

IDIOM OF JOY-AGE

ISLANDS BEYOND YESTERDAY. The people who live on the little lonely atolls of Micronesia in the very deep Pacific seem to live in Space-without-Time. They are insulated and isolated from the high-pressure, gadget-ridden life of our Contemporary Civilization by distance and delayed news. Current periodicals are from one to three months late. News is filtered and thinned. It is not *"news of what is happening"* but *"news of what happened and is past."* It loses impact through delayed time. These people seem to live by rhythms of sequence of events, the coming and going of schools of fishes, the blossoming and fruitage of trees and plants, the recurrence of feast days and holidays. Age sits lightly upon them because they do not count the years.

THEY GIVE LITTLE HEED to that Slave-Driver, Time, cracking the whip of *"hurry, hurry, hurry, it's later than you think."* These people of the Islands Beyond Yesterday believe that it is also "earlier than you think." They have considered the lily, how it grows, and they grow likewise.

OUR ISLANDS BEYOND YESTERDAY, in Idiom of Joy-Age, are areas of our own consciousness where we are insulated and isolated by meditation and contemplation of our Oneness with the One Consciousness, from the clamorous insistencies of John Ego Adamsmith's Hurry-go-round and from Romeo Lancelot Hamm's egotistical mouthings and bleatings.

ONLY AS WE FORGET TO REMEMBER that in our Veritable Consciousness, or Christ-Consciousness, *we are immortal now* do we seem to be a *part apart,* an island vulnerable to storm, typhoon, drouth and tidal wave.

LET US BE MERMEN for a little. Let us use our wonderful imaginations and have fun. We'll stand off from ourselves, or rather, we'll *swim off* from ourselves, and regard the island of Self, emergent above water. There it is. Individual. Now let's dive, deep, deep and deeper, until we know unforgettably that there is no separation; the base is joined with Earth. We are not alone. We are *not* a *part apart.* It's a great feeling.

WHOM I CALL FATHER

Who was my father? He was . . . *wait* . . . a Man?
  The gardener is not father of the seed
  He plants in answer to a primal need.
The gardener is an atom in the Plan
Vaster than his, or any mind, can span;
  Obeying orders of a greater Creed.

This gardener was entrusted with a grain,
  Seed of a seed of a seed's unbroken line,
  To plant in soil-of-flesh, *chance or design?*
It matters not. Flesh-soil harrowed with pain
Produced new seed, to link anew the chain,
  That for the moment waits in this life of mine.
Who was my father? He was a man . . . and good.
But he and I were sons of . . . *Fatherhood.*

UNIVERSAL HEART

Go where you will . . . to the uttermost part
Of Earth . . . you will find that each man has a heart;
It's the *same sort of heart* that is beating within
Whatever the tongue or the tint of the skin,
The same aching heart feels the sword-thrust of sorrow,
The same trusting heart births new hope for tomorrow.
The gestures will differ in multiple fashions
To express the same yearnings, the dreams and the passions.
The multiple gods will be sought and entreated
In multifold ways; and the sun will be greeted
With dances and rituals as varied as races,
But whatever the costumes, the tints of the faces,
Go where you will . . . to the uttermost part
Of Earth . . . you will find that each man has a heart.
And the language of heartbeats to all hearts is known;
To yours and to mine . . . *for no heart beats alone.*

BEYOND DROUTH

Dig past the *senses'* shallow surface earth
   Where sparkling springs deceive with proffered sips
Of transient *pleasure,* bubbles of bright mirth
   That leave the salt of thirst within the lips.
Dig past the strata yielding *happiness;*
   That fitful freshet-flood is quick to cease.
The tongue that knew its taste refuses less
   And parches more as quenching draughts decrease.

Dig deep if you would find the constant flow
   Of clear artesian waters, beyond drouth.
There are cool depths that lie serene below,
   Where Joy awaits the eager thirsting mouth.

LANDED GENTRY

He said, "I own ten thousand acres there
   From that high hill down to the ocean's shore.
   Within the year I'll own ten thousand more."
His manner hinted that he owned the air
   Through which we flew above his acred land.
   He guided the plane's swift flight with expert hand.

Some small unseen defect within the plane
   Brought us to earth with swift and stricken flight;
   His eyes that briefly gloried in the sight
Of land possessed closed beyond joy or pain.
   The land that held his transient throne dethroned him;
   Six feet of earth *he claimed he owned* now *owned him.*

And now he lies in his Futility Acres with an ornate monument shouting
in syllables of sculptured silence his frustrated ambition and his arrogant Will-to-Possess.

TREE TEMPERAMENTS

Aspen trees are flutter trees,
Billie-Burke-ing in the breeze.
　Pine are sigh-and-mutter trees,
　Thoughts-too-sad-to-utter trees.
Willow trees are weepy trees,
Ghostly, rather creepy trees.
　Hemlock trees are sleepy trees,
　Firs are Indian tepee trees.

Oaks are strong-and-sturdy trees,
Elms are nest-and-birdy trees.
　Palms are feather-duster trees.
　Redwoods are robuster trees.
Cherry trees are dainty trees,
Autumn maples . . . painty trees.
　Dogwood trees are springtime trees;
　Orange . . . wedding-ring-time trees.
But *any* trees, by canine measure,
Were grown for their especial pleasure.

THE PASSING SHOW *for John Ego Adamsmith*

Out there beyond our eyes the Passing Show
Goes on as it has gone, as it will go
Through changeless Time from ancient changeless Past
With changing scenes and costumes, changing cast,
But with the same old plot, the same suspense,
With nothing really new save Audience.
And after fifty years we may begin
To wonder, *"Isn't this where we came in?"*

AS THYSELF. . . .

"Love thy neighbor as thyself."
Ah, gladly would I, Neighbor.
But *"Know thyself,"* the first command.
There is the search and labor.

The "I" of me is a mystery
Deep-hidden from my knowing.
The splendid "You" behind the you
Is like the pre-dawn's glowing.

Can I know you? Can you know me?
Or can we know each other?
The "I" of me and the "You" of you,
How can we find "Us," Brother?

With eyes we search the face, the lips,
For hints and clues in gestures,
The Self concealed yet half-revealed
Within the fleshly vestures.

Not with the eyes, the words, the hands,
Nor intellect's keen probing
Will we discover what we seek,
But in our hearts' disrobing,

The "I" of me and the "You" of you
Will reach with spirit's fingers
To find again that twinhood lost
Whose splendid memory lingers.

"Love thy neighbor as thyself." Ah, gladly would I, Neighbor.
But *"Know thyself"* the first command . . . *there is the strife and labor.*

The Purpose of the Joyous Journey to Joy-Age is To "Know Thyself," to "Know Myself." To recognize and experience the Veritable Self. When that is known, then there "is no death of those we love. Through our Veritable Selves we truly know each other." This "knowingness" is not lost through distance nor death.

CHAIN REACTION

Said Mrs. Black to Mrs. Blair,
"You see that couple over there?
They're seen together everywhere.
They seem such a congenial pair."

To Mrs. Blabb said Mrs. Blair,
"You see that couple over there?
They're seen together *everywhere.*
Could they be having an *affair?*"

Said Mrs. Blabb to Grace McSnare,
"You see that couple over there?
They go together everywhere.
They're having such a *wild affair.*
I do declare!"

To Madame Crabbe said Grace McSnare,
"You see that couple over there?
I don't know *how they ever dare*
To show themselves. Aren't they aware
How people stare? I do declare."

Meanwhile "that couple over there"
Met Mrs. Blair's condemning stare
And Grace McSnare's cold damning glare
As though they really *weren't* aware
That they were having an affair.
They weren't . . . and so they didn't care.

And so, Mrs. Blair and Mrs. Blabb and Grace McSnare and Madame Crabbe
developed corsages of stomach-ulcers from frustrated gossipitis.

If Heaven was peopled exclusively by the people
who assured me that they were going there . . .
I'd choose a more tropical atmosphere myself.
As I told the young G.I. . . . . *I hadn't thought.* We are legion.
But I did get the idea that Heaven was supposed to be
a place of constant, not fluctuant, Joy. And NOT *off there.*
I don't know why the phrase "Joy is an *inside* job" crystallized my
amorphous ideas into something acceptable to my understanding. Timing, perhaps, and the fact that the phrase had none of the connotations
which Deacon Broilen Roastem had left with me. Perhaps my deep desire, coupled with receptive research, had readied me for clarification. A
chain reaction of understanding started, and it has not ended.

JOY, as I understand it, is a state of dynamic serenity,
in which a sense of health, happiness, growth, abundance
and security is a conviction and realization stemming
from focus-of-awareness in the Veritable Self. It is
something one works at to achieve, it is a job, a discipline, an acquiescence, an acceptance, an awareness, a giving up of something transient
for something lasting. It is Veritable; it is *"here and now and within,"*
not *"yonder, problematical and intermittent."*

The phrase gave me the clue to the meanings of the Great Patrin of
our Greatest Guide. The New and Old Testaments which heretofore
had been obscure became radioactive with power and truth. My focus-
of-awareness shifted from the World of Appearances to the Veritable
World in which we live inwardly. I saw Modern Science confirming in
the Laboratory what the Ancients had known intuitively.

There is One Universe, One Power, One Consciousness.
We exist wholly within it. We are in no way a part apart.

I needed the sealing and annealing experience.

It came when I had given up hope of it.

Please turn back to page 29 and "I Died At Dawn."

DIAMONDS OR DIAPERS

George Mellen, of Honolulu, who was my boss and coach during the time when I was beginning to learn to write through the medium of advertising copy, told me:

"Don't try to *sell* anything until you believe in it for twenty feet in every direction. Whether it's Diamonds or Diapers that you're trying to sell, get so enthusiastic about them that you live, dream and breathe Diamonds or Diapers.

Saturate yourself in the ideas until you ooze them like a sponge.

Then squeeze yourself . . .

and give out!"

Would you try to *sell* the idea of Life Preservers if one had been thrown to you when you were drowning? Would you try to *sell* the idea of Road-Signs to Water-Holes if a sign-post had guided you when you were dying of thirst in the parching desert?

Would you try to *sell* the idea of Living More While You're Living if you had lost your life and then found that you had not truly lived it until you lost it?

Mine is not an "explaining" talent. There are splendid writers who have given their life work to books with the technique of prayer and the practical practice of living through the Power of the Presence of Creative God-Consciousness. At best I can hope only to "infect" you with a desire to *experience for yourself* the increased Joy-of-Living which comes from the discovery of your Veritable Self.

I experienced the parching thirst for something more real than the waters-of-illusion of John Ego Adamsmith's transient world.

I was drowning hopelessly in the rip-tides and maelstroms of the emotions and intellectual confusions of John Ego Adamsmith's world. And I was dying from too much false-living which is John Ego Adamsmith's conception of life.

My thirst was a fever in my throat which became more parching with years. My hunger grew as I fed it pictures of food instead of the Bread of Life. The days of my living seemed to die as the flow of a stream is lost in the sands of the desert.

Three times it seemed that there was only one of two things to do . . . to go *out* or go *up*. I had too much curiosity about life to go *out*.

There was one course only, "Go up . . . Seeker."

→

The young G.I. (or you) might say, *"This book is supposed to be about 'Joy' but there's a lot of talk about sorrow, grief, pain, hardship."*
Let me tell you about the young chap who wanted an interview about "How he could become a writer." He came to my studio.
I was working on a prose book. I use teletype rolls of paper with carbon and second-sheets measuring yards and rods and even blocks long. I stick these yardages to the wall with thumbtacks where I can see them easily and not lose single sheets when the maid finds them on the floor and uses them for kitty-paper.
"So you want to be a writer?" I asked the young chap.
"Yep. Sounds like a career I'd like," he said expansively.
"Do you want to *work* at being a writer?" I asked.
"What do you mean *work?* Your stuff sounds as though you just burped it up . . . like writing letters."
I pointed to the yardages of manuscript on the wall. "I'm revising and retyping that . . . *all of it* . . . for the fourth time. Two hundred pages . . . to smooth out the knots and wrinkles and get that "burped up" effect that you like."
"Gosh!" he said. A soft plop indicated that his ambition had folded its wings and fallen to the floor.
Of course there's work, patience, discipline, failure, discouragement, hopelessness, renewed hope and work again in discarding John Ego Adamsmith and realizing Veritable Self.
There are Spiritual Growing Pains as well as Physical Growing Pains. Does the singer in his moment of triumph at the Metropolitan begrudge the hours of vocalization? Does the mountain climber want the easy peak? Calvary was not a stroll. We must reconcile ourselves to some equivalent of the Way of the Cross in our Search for Heaven, even though it is *within*.
But it is worth it. Every weary step of it.
If one person tells me that this book has helped, even a little, I will forget the hours of typing, erasings, self-doubt, the misunderstandings of my motives and the stress-and-strain of *living these* experiences in order to pass-them-along.

IDIOM OF JOY-AGE

SILENT PARTNER TALKS WITH JOHN EGO ADAMSMITH

"Adam" for race. "Smith" for family. "John" for individual. "Ego" for personality.

Silent Partner says, "John Ego Adamsmith,
The dust on the windowpane
Which makes you see 'as through a glass darkly'
Is your intellectual 'belief *in* God'
Instead of 'believing God'
Or experiencing 'God-Consciousness.'
    To 'believe *in* God'
    Is to regard God at a distance.
    When you experience God-Consciousness
    You realize
    That *in* God and *of* God
    You wholly live, move and have your only being,
    Without separation."
Silent Partner says, "John Ego Adamsmith,
Your persistence in making God in *your* image
Prevents your realization
That in your Veritable Self
You, the Veritable Man, are made in God's image and likeness.
    A man may know all there is to be known
    About water
    Yet die of thirst.
    A man may know all that is written and spoken about **God**
    Yet perish
    For lack of the experience of God-Consciousness."
Silent Partner says, "John Ego Adamsmith,
There is nothing you can tell God about yourself,
But there is much that you can learn about your Veritable Self
By listening.
    This Truth will not only make you free,
    But it will make you know that you are free."

THE SPIRIT OF FOREST LAWN

Written at the request of Colonel Eaton to express his ideal of the purpose of Forest Lawn. Most cemeteries are sad Futility Acres trying to perpetuate artifically what can be preserved only in the heart. By making Forest Lawn beautiful in every aspect, the lingering pain of the grim machinery of death with its aftermath is anesthetized by the balm of Beauty.

These things I would speak
Through the Silent Eloquence of Beauty;
  I, the Spirit of Forest Lawn, tell you
  That Shadows speak not of Darkness
  But of the Golden Light that cast them;
That Night is only the Shadow of Tomorrow
Going ahead to say, "I come . . . I am on my Way."
  That Sorrow says, "I could not be
  Where Love has never been.
  Rejoice and declare, 'I loved.'
That Memories are only the bright Dreams of Today
Moved into Yesterday by Tomorrow.
  Build new bright Dreams
  That you may have golden Memories."

**** **** **** ****

In John Ego Adamsmith's world, people die,
Friendships fail, fortunes crash,
Cyclones and earthquakes destroy homes,
Fine people seem to have the toughest luck,
While rat-people and cockroach-people seem to thrive.
  The world, seen through the eyes of Veritable Self, is different,
  Not a different world, but a different *seeing* of the world,
  Not a different world, but a different living in this world.
  A Great Guide showed us the way,
  Why haven't we followed?

LESS THAN THE FLOWER

I challenged a flower, "Show me God."
The petals, the leaves, the root, the clod
Cried out, "What proof *is* proof to eyes
Which can not see when the *answer* lies
Within and *before* the eyes that seek?
Would you have a Voice of Thunder speak?
  Must the Burning Bush burst into flame?
  Let your anguished Heart cry out the Name,
Then wait for the radar-answer clear,
"Not *there,* afar, but here . . . *here* . . . *here.*"
  The root, the clod, the leaf, the rose . . .
  Can we know less than a flower knows?

THE CONSIDERED LILY

I heeded the admonition, "Consider the lily . . . how it grows!"
At first, my thoughts were busy with the form, beauty and detail
of the blossom emerging from its green sheathing.
    Then a stillness grew between us.
In that stillness the lily told me, "As the immaterial but real blossom-
to-be is within me, shaping, forming, unfolding, pressing out in obedi-
ence to an invisible but real blueprint in the sheath of me,
    so is the Emergent or Veritable Self of *you*
    shaping, forming, unfolding, pressing out
    within the sheath of your fleshly envelope
    and the atmosphere of your human personality."
Actually, neither the bulb of the lily nor the sheath of flesh of myself
or yourself "contains" the Emergent Blossom or Veritable Self. The
fleshly bulb, either plant or human, is the tangible or exteriorized expression of the *immaterial but real* Organizing Field which is magnetic from
the physicist's viewpoint, or spiritual from the mystical, spiritual or
metaphysical viewpoint. This Organizing Field or Genii (read Gustaf
Stromberg's splendid book, "Soul of the Universe," for scientific con-

→

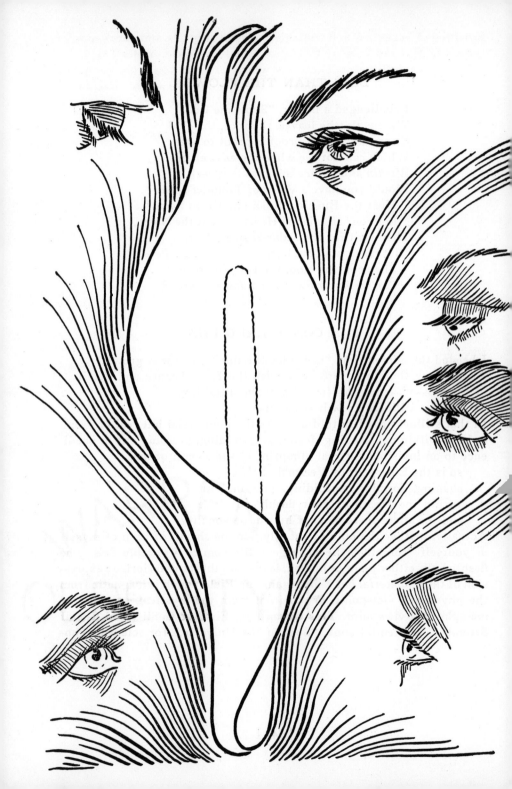

firmation) * organizes and controls the emerging life and expression of the individualized unit of Universal Creative Consciousness, God.

If any words have connotations which prevent you from accepting them without prejudice, *do not use them for a while.* Use terms which are *"comfortable in your mind."* Words are only verbal capsules containing meanings but are in no wise *that-which-is.*

Walk softly when the small-mighty Voice speaks within.
Let not the crackle of a twig of anxiety
nor the whisper of your excited breath
nor the soft drums of your heart
mute the syllables of that speaking.
Wait, acquiescent and receptive. . . .
  It is always speaking . . . listen *now.*

THE TATTOOED MAN

The Tattooed Man unveiled his epidermal scrap-book of pictures for the delight of the circus crowd. Toe to top-knot, pictures!

Small Boy yipped his question, "Mama, was the man born with all of those pictures on him?"

Mama said, "No. If he could scrub them off you'd see the real man underneath all of this tattooing."

We are born with our individual pattern of self. At once we are taken over by parents, teachers, family, books, environment, associations, experiences and *tattooed* with preferences, prejudices, fears, superiorities and inferiorities.

Meditation, study, prayer-of-listening, alerted awareness self-examination . . . these are the neutralizers of the inks of such tattooing. With persistence we may find our Veritable Selves under the epidermal scrap-book of personality.

Until then we might well echo Small Boy's question. "Was I born with all of these pictures on me?"

* Incidentally, read the Appendices first, then backtrack to the beginning.

DARE SPEAK OF JOY

You may well ask, "How dare you speak of Joy
In a world where men feed brothers' flesh to swine,
And demagogues inflame themselves with wine
Drained from the veins of men; when gray alloy
Of lies is specious coin that Nations use
To buy and sell the armaments of Power?
How dare you speak of Joy in this red hour
When monster-minds ride death-winds to diffuse
The germs of Hate across a stricken Earth?
Can you say "Joy" when dark corrosive Grief
Riddles the human heart, when thug and thief
Lead the Parade? This is no time for Mirth."

I do not talk of Mirth . . . nor Happiness . . .
When hurricanes of Fear disperse the stars,
When Truth is locked behind the man-made bars
Of lies, lies, lies; when dirges of Distress
Blend with atomic bombs to detonate,
To ravel the mind and deafen listening ears.
Not Happiness when deluges of tears
Render the salt sea salter, when stark Hate
Drives Crucifixion-nails into the palms
Of hands uplifted to the smog-gray skies;
Not Happiness . . . when tears blur frantic eyes
And hungering hearts must feed on Sorrow's alms.

I dare to speak of Joy and cry that word
Because of One who knew Golgotha's Cross,
Who drained the bitterest Cup, and knew the dross,
The scourge, the dregs. Out of the night I heard
A Voice cry "Joy" when my own heart cried "Grief."
My mind refused; my senses would not hear,
But in my heart the Call rang trumpet-clear,
"Lo, I am with you alway." My belief
Rose like the soldiers who with broken knees
Crawl with the flag to place it on the hill;

Crawl as they watch their pulsing red blood spill
From their own veins. *Shall we be less than these?*

Christ, with the Cross in his clairvoyant gaze,
   Cried "Joy" in nights as black as these we know;
   Cried "Joy" to the lepers, bidding them to go
Healed into life . . . and gave the blind new days.
I dare to speak of "Joy" because I know
   That One who knew the Cross knew Joy despite
   Gethsemane, and agony of the night,
And dread of the long harsh road which He must go.
His was a promise given. I accept.
   And when the mind betrays me with its fright
   I will turn blinded eyes . . . and find the Light,
And cry with Joy to find that Promise . . . kept!

A woman in an audience had protested, "How can you speak of Joy in times like these?"

John Ego Adamsmith and Jane Ego Evesmith, in their humanness, speak of Pleasure, Happiness, Delight. Jesus, with Christ vision, speaks of Joy. Joy is the immortal, inexhaustible out-pouring of the Veritable Self. All of the great creative forces of life come from this source, the God-Consciousness. They are not *generated* by John Ego Adamsmith; but when John Ego Adamsmith is *regenerated* by the rebirth which comes from moving the focus-of-awareness from his human Seeming-Self into the Veritable Self, these forces reshape his life. They do not have to be *sought;* they are *released.*

When we search for *God outside ourselves* we are like a deep-sea fish frantically swimming from the Atlantic to the Pacific to the Arctic and to the Antarctic, looking for Ocean.

Be still and *know.* Be still and *realize.* Be still and *experience that-which-you-are,* your Veritable Self.

DARE SPEAK OF JOY

This poem could not have been written with conviction if there had not been an experience so real, so complete that no argument could prevail against it, nor could subsequent "times of fog" do more than transiently dim the Authority of it.

In the blackest hour of all my living, when the human mind's clever arguments were straw timbers for the House of my Security, I turned intuitively to *I-knew-not-what* and *I-knew-not-where* as a frightened child in the night cries out for the assurance of Mother or Father to drive away the *"scare-things"* of nightmare.

Wordlessly and thought-lessly I cried out. The cry was more desperate because there were no words nor sounds, only the mute plea of a heart stripped of all defenses, all prides, all brave futile pretenses.

And wordlessly and thought-lessly the Answer came. But it came *not* from "out there," but from *within,* a deep artesian uprush of courage as calm and still as the water in the Filled Cup, yet as mighty as the typhoon winds of the Deep Pacific.

The experience can not be explained nor conveyed in words. I can only refer to the poem, "I Died At Dawn" as an inadequate statement of the timeless moment.

I can only say, "I testify . . . that there *is* a Presence, there *is* a Way, there *is* an Answer . . . and there will always be the Promise . . . kept."

STRIPPED ARMOR

How thirstily the life-worn Heart desires
   The quenching cold of high unsullied snow
On sky-thrust peaks to ease the fevered fires
   When lust flames of Youth have burned too low,
   And cindered sullen embers dully glow
Before the final wistful spark expires.

Better to climb the stark forbidding path
   To cloud-shrined heights on bleeding wounded feet
And mount through guardian storms' defending wrath
   To clean fulfilling death; to know, complete,
   What strips the Heart of armored flesh to meet
A Quested Faith . . . *sans* gray aftermath.

QUESTION AND ANSWER IN KOREA

Is this the black ultimate answer . . . death . . . decay?
That which was once a man is not a man.
It is a shattered vessel, crumbling clay
  Dissolving soddenly, ending its transient span
As flesh-container for the fluid breath
  That flowed from *where-and-when* into this hour
From dim beginnings. *Does this end in death?*
  Where has it gone . . . the heart's strong pulsant power?

This was the vessel only. Give the shards
  Compassionate and quick return to earth.
Moisten the clay with tears. Life but discards
  The Temporary Cup of fragile worth.
Finger the cold familiar curves, and *know*
  They were for mind's and senses' brief employ.
The Wine of Life flows on . . . will ever go
  To new-formed Cups, brimming with deathless Joy.

WHY DO WE MOURN?

Why do we mourn the summer's going,
  The fading of a flower?
Tears are proof of the Heart's unknowing
  That in the blossom's hour
The Fruitage waits on the petal's falling . . .
  Not Death but a glad Release,
Freeing the seed to follow the Calling. . . .
  In the Harvest the Heart finds Peace.

True, but it still hurts when a lovely thing seems to die
until we understand. . . .

THE LIGHT IS MINE

Gray day. Gray sky. The slow sad drip of rain.
Gray twilight filming on the windowpane.
The shadows stir with ghosts. The wincing nerves
Shrink from the Waiting Cup that coldly curves
To shape a gray jade cup, a thirsting hollow
That bids me fill with tears . . . and wryly swallow.

But I refuse. One small brave candle's light
Will valiantly defend me from the night.
There is the open hearth, good wood to burn,
The air is filled with music if I turn
The radio's quick dial . . . and lacking these
I have my thoughts, to haunt me or to tease
My grieving heart back into ways of Joy.
I'll light the Heart's bright flame, burn the alloy
Of grayness from Life's gold and make it fine.
The shadows are the Night's . . . the Light is Mine.

LITTLE LESSER GODS

I worshipped Little Lesser Gods
    Until I found that they were clay.
The Rain of Time dissolved the clods.
    The Winds of Chance blew them away.
And I was lost . . . and I was lost
    With Little Lesser Gods away.
I modeled New Ones at the cost
    Of blood to mix the pliant clay.
But blood and tears . . . and sodden clods
Make only Little Lesser Gods.

IS IT THAT EASY?

"I'll light the Heart's bright flame . . . The Light Is Mine."
Is it as easy as that?
>Yes, it is as easy as flooding a dark room with light
>by pulling a switch.
>But, ah! *Finding the light-switch in a darkened room!*
It is as easy as opening a door by turning a key in the lock.
>But, ah! *Finding the right key on the key-ring in the dark!*
That is John Ego Adamsmith's problem. Your problem. My problem.
With our focus-of-awareness in the Flesh and the Intellect we are
fumbling in the dark for the light-switch or the right key.
>In our Veritable Selves we *are* the Light.
>Our Lord-Consciousness is the Key, the Door . . . and Freedom.
>Our Christ-Consciousness is the Way.
By the power of muscle-strength we try to storm Heaven. We try with
arrogant will-power to gain mastery. We have achieved wonders.
>We have conquered all but our Lesser Selves.
>We gain mastery of all but our Lesser Selves.
>Our Lesser Selves sell us to the Enemy. The rebels. Traitors.
We offer the blood and tears and sodden clods of our Flesh
on the altars of the Little Lesser Gods of John Ego Adamsmith.
Always when we lift our faces in expectancy of an answer . . .
The Rains of Time and the Winds of Chance have dissolved them . . .
And blown them away as dust.

**** **** **** ****

The Boy-Next-Door yells, *"Mrs. Jones, is Willie home?"*
Mrs. Jones, *"Yes, Bobby, Willie is home."*
The Boy-Next-Door, *"Can Willie come out and play?"*
Mrs. Jones says, *"Willie has to stay in. He's been naughty. He's sick."*
or *"Yes, Bobby, Willie may come out and play."*
>"Willie" is our inner *Joy.* Willie is home.
>Places, people, things, sunsets, spring, moonlight, music, love, scenery,
a hundred things hourly call, *"Can Joy come out and play?"*
>Only we can say or may say, *"Joy . . . run out and play."*
And Willie-Joy is always busting to run out and play.

DIVIDED ROAD

I passed the Halfway House some time ago.
  The People said, "The Road goes *down* from here . . .
  The Easy Road." I saw it wind and veer
In ever-gentling curves, placid and slow,
Down to the meadow lands, the valley floor
  With flat monotony of hill-less plains
  Away from storms, blessed by the tempered rains
Where distance mutes the avalanche's roar
And veils of blueness blur the jagged lines
  Of high peaks challenging the tired heart.
  There is a world below, remote, apart
From stressed desires. The fruitage of the vines
Hangs easy to the hand in listless wealth
  Where Indian Summer's languor lingers long,
  And there is lulling rhythm of slow song
As days and hours pass with tiptoe stealth.

I passed the Halfway House some time ago.
  The Road divides. The Easy Road goes down.
  The Rugged Path leads to the snowy crown
Of distant peaks. The siren land below
Offers the weary body soft delights
  Spread out like viands of a languid feast.
  My Mountain Heart, like some wild wary beast,
Turns from the baited trap . . . to seek the Heights.

THEN YOU KNOW

When you look at a star
And it is not far;
When the song of a bird
Is your own heart stirred
To voice its note
In the bird's soft throat;
When you feel and know
That the ebb and flow
Of the sea's salt flood
Is your rhythmed blood;
When a flower blooms
And its sweet perfumes
Distil in your heart
As the petals part;
When Life and you
    In flesh or clod
Are One . . . not two . . .
    Then you know God.

LAST ROAD-SIGN ON THE JOYOUS JOURNEY
TO JOY-AGE

Fill the Waiting Cup of the Expectant Hour
with your own inexhaustible artesian Joy-of-Living,
since you drink the draught that you yourself have poured.